THE
Secret
IS OUT

A MEMOIR

DR. ALICIA MICHELLE SIMPSON

Copyright © 2024

The Secret is Out
Dr. Alicia Michelle Simpson
Publication Date: August 17, 2024
Printed in the U.S.A.

Becoming 50Something Publications
Email: 50somethinglifestyle@gmail.com
ISBN: 979-8-218-47930-5

Dedication

God is Faithful! I dedicate this project to my husband, Keith, and my three sons: Gregory, Austin, and David; and my grandchildren, Ayala, Hannah Mia, Olivia and Cody. Lastly, but certainly not least, my parents, Charles and Genevieve, who inspired me to always do my best. I could never have completed this massive project without the constant encouragement from my two sisters, who departed this life too soon, H. Tucker Watkins and Catherine Beverely Benjamin. These two ladies listened while I wept, screamed, and wanted to give up. This book could not have been possible without them. My sister Beverly started out with me and was able to provide responses to chapters one and two. I am equally grateful to my niece, Leah Benjamin, who stepped in to help with scriptural research for chapters five–seven. I am grateful and honored for every person who, like Moses, stood on either side of me at certain times of my crossing of the Red Sea and my journey through Egypt to help me hold up my arms to see me through.

Foreword

E. Geneva Conway

I have known Alicia all of her life. Her family were great contributors to the church we all attended. Her life has been hills, valleys and mountains, but she trusted God and in His Word. This book is her testimony, one of many. This book will be very helpful to anyone who thinks their problems are insurmountable. I pray you will be blessed by, not only the words of the pages, but the unique formatting of the book which she provides scriptural references. Most, but not all of the scriptural references provide in-depth narrative of how she became free of the struggle; the secret she held for years. As you read the following pages, adopt and embrace your closely kept secret, while learning how to be free of the emotional bondage that has consumed you for way too long.

Contents

Foreward: E. Geneva Conway ii

Prelude..1

Chapter One:How It Started...........................6

Chapter Two: A Way Out...............................13

Chapter Three: Prince Charming.....................23

Chapter Four: Detours and Determination...........27

Chapter Five: Taking Charge..........................33

Chapter Six: The Birth 39

Chapter Seven: Jumping the Broom......................44

Chapter Eight: On the Run 52

Chapter Nine: I've Had Some Good Days................60

Chapter Ten: I've Had Some Hills to Climb 67

Chapter Eleven: Sleepless Nights 75

Chapter Twelve: Breaking Point 80

Epilogue..87

About the Author......................................89

For there is nothing covered that will not be revealed, nor hidden that will not be known. Therefore, whatever you have spoken in the dark will be heard in the light, and what you have spoken in the ear in inner rooms will be proclaimed on the housetops.

Luke 12: 2-3

Prelude

Albany, New York, and another cold and blustery day. My shift was ending soon, and I was looking forward to going home. Home was a little distance from work—20 miles, to be exact. Working thirteen-hour days was not only long, but by working in the hospital, it could be daunting. Sick patients required so much care and understanding. As a respiratory therapist, I not only dealt with the sick patient but the families too.

As respiratory therapists, we were often pulled in many different directions during our shifts: the patients we saw on the main floors, the patients we cared for in the ICU, and let's not forget the many emergencies we attended when appointed to work in the emergency room. Unlike our nursing counterparts, we did not only work on one floor, but rather we provided care everywhere except the morgue, for one twelve-hour shift.

My tenure as a respiratory therapist, better known as a RT, ended when I was offered the opportunity to step into a role as a pulmonary function technician. How exciting this was! I was no longer required to work those ghastly twelve-hour shifts, making for a sixteen-hour day with driving to and from work and getting up at four in the morning. People would say that I should be happy because we only worked three days a week. Well, it always felt like much more than that. In my new position, I was working eight hours a day!

This was the life. I had my own office full of medical equipment needed to operate an efficient pulmonary lab for all the tests ordered by the patient's pulmonologist. This area of care was busy, just not as many hours as in my previous position. During one shift in the lab, I would perform between six to ten various types of tests. The medical testing included performing a breathing test inside a PFT (pulmonary function test) box to help the physician definitively confirm and diagnose asthma, emphysema, exercise induced asthma, blood oxygen levels, and more. Testing, depending on the ordered test, took anywhere from forty-five minutes to three hours per patient visit.

Working in this position required concentration, teaching skills, and the aptitude to understand the types of tests and how to administer them for exceptional quality outcomes for proper diagnosis. Pulmonologists were known to come into the lab at least one to two times a week to read the outcomes of the tests and make life-changing diagnoses. The day consisted of managing both inpatients (those already admitted to the hospital) and outpatients alike). I kept and adhered to a strict schedule. I would not want to have the sicker inpatients wait in the waiting room while taking care of the outpatients. I was working as if I were in private practice.

Managing appointments was not all I had to do. I also provided information and instructions for the appointments, then confirmed them. This was necessary to maintain the required flow for the day for the revolving patients. Alongside these components of managing the lab, I was also able to provide a shoulder to cry on. The days were long. The work was important.

Concentration was becoming increasingly difficult. My focus was shifting from my patients to my home life. My life was debilitated. I understood the patient's illnesses and, in most cases, why the patient suffered from lung disease. More importantly, I understood how difficult their lives were becoming. My home life, on the other hand, was not so easy to understand. What was happening? I was unable to make a clear decision as to what caused the once healthy home life I was enjoying to become debilitated and unstable. Life was spiraling out of control.

During the snowy and blustering days in Upstate New York, my husband of eighteen years, insisted on driving me to work. My husband had busy days. He was attending outpatient NA meetings as often as he could to recover from an unfortunate drug abuse problem that caused him to lose his prestigious position with a well-known pharmaceutical company. Because we were down to one car, I wanted to ensure that Greg would be able to have the care he needed to return to being a solid citizen of society. In order to accomplish this, I would need to trust him to pick me up from work.

No one at work really knew what I was going through or my daily family challenges. All they really knew was that I was excellent at what I did and that the patients and pulmonologist loved and respected me. Working in the pulmonary lab office was often a very lonely place. The fifteen windows and all the light that came in during the day did not create the warmth I expected.

I tried to remember to eat lunch and enjoy a few breaks with my former respiratory buddies as often as possible. These were always happy times. Times that I did not have to think about being picked up or not being picked up by Greg. For a few brief minutes, I was able to have peace of mind talking about current events and detailing the choicest recipes. The laughter was such a welcoming interlude. However, that time did not last long. More patients were expected to arrive meaning my intermission was over. It was time to go back to work.

On this particular day, after lunch, there was a shift in my emotions. The shift in my once peaceful outlook was quickly changing to anxiousness and doubt. I became anxious about Greg not coming to pick me up after work again. From this point on in the day, I began to watch the clock with one eye. I could hear each precise tick and Swiss movement of the wall clock. My heart followed the sound and sank lower and lower. "He has to pick me up on time," I uttered to myself. Otherwise, the secret might come out.

Once my last patient left, I began to close up shop. I worked slowly and steadily, not wanting to be aware of how much time had elapsed. I was there longer than I should have been, much longer than I needed to be. I hurried and closed the door to the office. I was careful to be as quiet as possible. No one could know I was still at work two hours after my shift. What words could I use to explain why I was still there? This was overwhelming. I just needed to talk to someone. Someone had to console me.

Another hour passed. No call. I continued to dial Greg's cell number. praying perhaps he had overslept. Maybe he mistakenly left his phone at home because he was in such a rush to come get me. Of course, none of these things could be true because he was now three and one-half hours late! Anxiety was giving way to anger, regret, and depression. I care for people all day. Who cares for me? I needed to talk to someone. I needed help.

I decided to make a call to the Crisis Hotline. Surely, they would listen and be consoling. I made the call, and on the other end of the line was a very congenial and soothing voice. I was asked how they could help. I said, "I don't want to be here anymore." With my head in my hand and my eyeballs swimming in a flood of tears, I looked up. To my disappointment, I saw a sight that is usually only seen on television.

Entering the room were the nursing house supervisor, two hospital security guards, and two police officers. I knew then that I could no longer hide behind the façade. The secret was out.

Part One

I KNOW GOD

Chapter One
How it Started

I was born in the summer of 1959 to Genevieve and Charles Tucker. I was the fourth and last child born to this union. I have three older siblings: two sisters and one brother. My oldest sister is fifteen years older than me; my second oldest sister is fourteen years older than me; and my brother is almost nine years older. I really am the baby of the family.

I have always considered myself to be a very giving and nurturing person. I always want to help wherever I can. Helping people has always been my focus. I became this way because I found out a long time ago that by not concentrating on my own problems or situations, it would help me immensely. So, I began to think of others and put my issues on the back burner.

Growing up, I was somewhat of a loner. While I had siblings, they were not at home with me, except for my brother Marshall. My sisters were away at college. By the time I started kindergarten, both had already finished junior college and were on their way to university. My oldest sister, Harriet, would enter the State University of New York at Albany, while my sister Beverly went away to college to attend Buffalo State College. Both were enrolled in education, desiring to become extraordinary elementary school educators. My brother, Marshall, was still in high school.

So, here I was, left behind if you will, without really getting to know my sisters because of the age gap and living with my mom, dad, and brother. I remember my sister Beverly calling home and making a collect call. Yes, I answered a landline phone and spoke with a telephone operator. I usually answered the phone and said, "Hi, yes, I will accept the collect call." I handed the phone over to my mom who was usually sewing and chewing gum. Sewing was her current career, as she was a stay-at-home mom.

We lived in the projects; a twelve-story high rise to be exact with an incinerator in the common area to dispose of our trash. We lived in Apt. 2A and Mama Cade, my grandmother, lived in 2D. The youth choir director, Sis. Freeman lived next door to us in 2B. A pastor and his wife, the Jacksons, lived in the last apartment on the second floor opposite my home. They had no children.

The second floor was blessed. Our apartment was the largest unit on the floor. We had five bedrooms and two full bathrooms, a family style living room that was large enough for us to all sit comfortably and watch our black and white television. We often watched television together.

Each of us had our own bedroom. My brother's room was the first room after the kitchen around the corner. My parents' room was next to his. The room was full of matching off-white furniture and a free-standing Singer sewing machine with scraps of material and different colored remnants of thread. A tape measure hung on the back of mom's chair, which she never pushed in, and a host of straight pins with the colored heads were stuffed into the pin cushion.

Rounding the corner, was where I resided. My room was always neat and tidy. My twin bed was adorned with a pink and white chenille bedspread. Around the perimeter of the room were my many doll babies, the crib that many were kept in, and the one doll I was afraid of that I stuffed in the corner. She was a four-foot-tall doll with moving eyes. She was the Christmas gift I didn't care for. I loved my room; it was my haven.

Beverly's room was next to mine, although she was only home during school vacations and summer breaks. I recall her room having lots of blue, her favorite color. No one went in there; it was like a museum until she arrived and brought life to the 10 x 10 space. The last room belonged to my sister, Harriet. This was an interesting situation. Harriet was a student at Albany Law School and lived in the public library from after class until the library closed at 10 p.m. Because of the hours she kept, my dad decided that Harriet should have the largest and last room in the house. This was a unique situation because this was a suite. This room housed a private half-bath. I hardly ever saw my sister because I was the generation that went to bed promptly at 8:30, tired or not, every season of the year. Hence, summertime was no different. Homework was done before this time and ready to be handed in the next day. This was also the place where, on Saturday nights, I studied my Sunday school lesson.

The lessons in the book included questions with fill-in-the blanks. I was always prepared to answer and ask questions in Sunday school. This is when I learned to appreciate and study God's word.

Growing up my mom was a personal seamstress for a few people. Two ladies were of particular interest to me. I recall thinking they were interesting people because they did not live in the projects. They were not even black. They were rich, white Jewish women. I distinctly recall two women, Mrs. Mandelbaum and Mrs. Whitfield. I'm not sure what Mrs. Mandelbaum's claim to fame was, but I knew for sure that Mrs. Whitfield was the prominent wife of a neurosurgeon. There seemed to always be another fitting at the house.

While I remember Mrs. Whitfield being very petite and thin, with a strong southern accent, what I remember most about her is that she called my mother Genevieve. I didn't like that, but I wasn't sure why. Why did we call her Mrs. Whitfield but she didn't call my mom Mrs. Tucker? The more I questioned my mother about this, the more trouble I got into. I was told it was respectful to call her by her last name, because that is how things were. I think this is when, at seven, I became a social activist. Wanting to ensure equal rights for all people. This is when I discovered that all people were not treated equally, and white people were viewed as superior. That could only make me one thing: inferior. I needed to make a change.

I was in fact making a change. Not for equal rights, but for personal rights. My relationship with my mom was strained. We never got along well; we never saw things in the same light. While growing up in the church, my mother was very active in many areas. She, as mentioned earlier, taught Sunday school, was a member of the Sewing Circle, and had a role with the finance committee, which helped to support the weekly finances of the church. Her role in this endeavor was to account for the "tribe" leaders who collected money weekly and reported to my mom the total amount collected. The calling of roles, or the calling of each tribe leader, was the job of my mom.

My mother was also active in the senior choir. She would even lead songs from time-to-time. The church was a huge part of our lives. It was normal for our family to attend church several days a week: Sunday, Sunday night, Tuesday for Bible Band, Wednesday for Junior Church and Junior Church choir rehearsal, and Friday commonly referred to as pastoral night. The pastor would receive the offerings presented to the church on Friday nights. As I was growing up, the younger generation would deem this night "grocery shopping night" for the pastor and his wife, the First Lady. I not only learned a lot by attending church, but I also had fun, too.

Attending church so often and on a regular basis, caused me to be more sheltered than most children my age. I played four specific roles growing up in the housing projects: a teacher, a doctor, a missionary, and a wife and mom. I didn't play cards, which was considered a sin. I didn't play games with more than one dice, because the church believed gamblers played with two dice and gambling was a sin. I never learned how to play Chinese checkers because the leaders of the church, who had little to no education, misinterpreted scripture. Growing up, we were told that the scripture stated we should "marble," not because that too was a sin. In fact, the scripture actually says, "Marvel not that I said not thee, ye must be born again." This scripture is found in John 3:7. My personality was very challenging to many people, especially the people in the church. I asked a lot of questions. My asking questions was considered disrespectful. Hence, I should believe what people told me, simply because I was a child.

Well, I didn't just take everyone at their word, I still asked questions. Two pivotal things happened from this. The first being that the distance between me and my mom grew wider, and the second being that I was now more than thirsty for understanding the Word of God. I wanted to understand scripture for myself, not from man's interpretation. Now, I was really a stand-alone individual. I was viewed as atypical by my cousins and peers. Where most children listened intently to adults and believed every word they uttered, Alicia was considered confrontational and disrespectful simply because the responses I got did not connect the dots.

I certainly did not see things that way. I just simply wanted to understand. I was fascinated with the body and how it worked, as well as scripture. For me, there was a definite correlation between the two. I needed to know more, and I would not rest until I had answers to my many questions. Scientific questions such as how do my legs grow longer, and spiritual questions such as why we were not allowed to wear pants or go to the movies? I asked my mom these types of questions, and she always appeared unnerved by my asking. She could not answer the question I asked in fifth grade about how my legs grew longer, but she had a quick response for me when I asked why we could not wear pants.

Growing up in the northeast was challenging in the winter months and serene during other times. Because the weather was treacherous and I was required to stand at the bus stop to wait for the bus to get to school, I again questioned my mom about the wearing of pants. But this time, I presented a scenario. I asked her if Jesus would rather me have pneumonia and ask the church to pray for my healing, or would He prefer that I wear pants to be warm? I really cannot describe the look she gave, but it was hard to argue with the facts presented. I was able to wear pants from that time on.

The strain of cohabiting with my mom was becoming more intense. We always seemed to rub each other the wrong way. Even when, or at least I felt, I was doing my best to be cordial and "sweet," my mom didn't see things the way I saw them. To make matters worse for me, my parents decided to divorce when I was twelve years old. Once again, my childhood "smart mouth" raised its ugly head, and I asked my mom, "Why are you getting a divorce. You both are going to die soon, why not just stay married?" That obviously was not the appropriate thing to say, I guess. So, my life continued to spiral out of control for me. I could not believe that I was now going to be *held hostage* in my own home with only my mother and not my father! By this time, my brother had been accepted into Union College, in Schenectady, New York, and was living on campus. Hence, I was all alone in the house, suffering. At this point, loneliness had taken on a new dimension. All I could think of was that I had to get out of there.

At fourteen, I did just that. I ran away. I went to my girlfriend's house and called my dad to come get me, He lived in a neighboring city twenty miles away. I felt trapped. I felt like I was suffocating, and all the oxygen around me was being consumed at a rate that was insufficient for my survival. My dad, who had never raised his voice at me, calmly let me know he was on his way. Oh, how I adored my dad. He was indeed my first knight in shining armor. He was coming to rescue me from loneliness.

I stayed with my dad and stepmom, Ms. Marie, for two nights. What a reprieve from the living situation I was accustomed to. Everything was wonderful. I knew I was not going to be able to live with him, even if this is what I had been praying for. My mom and dad shared custody, but I had to live with her. I did, however, get to see my dad every weekend.

It was my Cinderella time on Saturdays to clean the entire house, while my dad sat outside in the car waiting for me. He always came to pick me up at noon, which I guess was the time my parents agreed to. However, my mom always found one more thing for me to do. One more inspection of what I had already cleaned and was now being scrutinized. My best efforts to do an amazing job cleaning, so I could be with my dad, seemingly did not pass inspection. The noon pickup time usually became 12:45–1:00, without fail. I never got to spend the night with my dad; I had to be home by 6:00 P.M. I remember saying the same thing over and over, "I got to get out of here."

Scriptural Response

ECCLESIASTES 12:1 (NIV)

Remember your Creator in the days of your youth, before the days of trouble come and the years approach when you will say, "I find no pleasure in them" (Ecclesiastes 12:1 NIV).

A child saved is a soul saved, plus a life.

I was the family's baby and was spoiled by all of the family. My family loved me, and I never gave them any reason to worry about my character or youthful motives. I was a typical child. In many ways, my family shared the perception of me being an adult beyond my years. I was focused, intelligent, determined, and much more knowledgeable about life than most people my age. When I made up my mind to do something, I did it, and I did it to my satisfaction.

One thing I did well was to dedicate my life to Christ, or, as I fondly call him, the Big Guy. For me and the family, church was essential to our everyday lives. Every Sunday, we were in Sunday school, then morning service. On Tuesdays, we attended Bible study. On Fridays, we returned to church for the weekly service. Saturdays were for youth group activities, including choir rehearsals and usher board meetings.

Our denomination was the Church of God in Christ, the most prominent Black Pentecostal denomination. This denomination sets aside two weekly days as fasting days. Members all over the world were encouraged to go without food or drink for a set time on those days and, as much as possible, consecrate themselves to the Lord. I decided, as a pre-teen, to participate in this activity.

I made this decision by myself to strengthen my relationship with the Lord. Somewhere in my spiritual development, I realized that my allegiance was to be with God in any and every way I could achieve that.

By putting God in a prominent place in my young life, I was affirming some critical spiritual truths: loving and worshiping God brings joy, peace, excitement, and abundance in indescribable and undeniable ways.

Was that my motivation? I doubt it. The Holy Spirit was drawing me in, and I was not resistant. I remember the scripture about the Good Shepherd. Most children know that story and have the picture of Jesus carrying the little lamb on His shoulders planted indelibly in their minds. I remember the verse in John 10:10 that reminds us that the Good Shepherd came into the world to offer us abundant life. After all, it's no secret that God wants us to be happy.

The genuinely remarkable fact about me is that I discovered much about God early in my life—before things got terrible. I was developing just the type of scaffold I would need when troubles came and things hit rock bottom, as they did.

Chapter Two
A Way Out

In 1974, at the age of fifteen I took on the largest endeavor to date. That was to volunteer to babysit for my second oldest sister, Beverly. Not only was this my way out, but I also wanted to do this because Beverly needed help. Beverly was thrown into the single-mom club due to a recent divorce. Not only was she recently divorced, but she was also working on her second master's degree in education. Beverly was not able to go to school, work full time, or pay for a babysitter on the salary of an elementary school teacher. So off I went to help with the rearing of my two nieces, Tamika, and Leah. I was out on parole.

Before I moved to Amherst, New York, a suburb of Buffalo, I lived in Albany, New York, and went to a very small private school, Milne. Milne was a part of the university system of the state that allowed the student teachers the chance to practice with the students before becoming certified teachers. I was very fortunate to be enrolled in this school. There was not only tuition associated with Milne but an entrance exam as well. The tuition was paid, and I did well enough to be accepted. This was good. Milne was in a very small and intimate setting. The building was older, yet it possessed a great deal of character. The stairs were worn but polished. The classroom doors were made of wood and very heavy. There was a chalkboard. On occasion, we would have an overhead projector to emphasize a special lesson. The school enrollment was about 500 students from grades nine to twelve. Milne was a very small school. I knew everyone in my class and most of the other students as well. I liked being there. I liked the intimacy it seemed to have.

Moving to Amherst to help my sister, on the other hand, was somewhat different. I was enrolled in a much larger institution with no apparent intimacy. In my second semester of tenth grade, I was to be a student at Sweet Home Senior High School, home of the Panthers. Sweet Home was like a city to me. It was big, it was crowded, and it was noisy. I certainly was no longer in Kansas, but I felt like I had transitioned to Oz.

While I was the new girl at school, many people were interested in getting to know me. One of those people was Gregory Giles. Gregory was very tall, quite handsome, polite, and very smart. I prided myself on being a good student. I loved to learn new things. I love to read. I was not, however, really interested in Gregory until I discovered that he knew more vocabulary words than I did. To me, this was very impressive. Although Gregory was very good with vocabulary, he lacked the ability to do math well. Finding out that I could do math and geometry at the time, he enlisted my help. Greg would meet me every morning at the designated spot in school prior to class starting and ask me for the homework. He did not want to be tutored; he just wanted to copy my work. Because I was new and he was six feet three, I gave him the assignment. Not only was Greg all the things I described above, but he was also a great athlete. He lettered at least three times. These three accomplishments included track, basketball, and football. Basketball was his favorite. He so wanted to be like Dr. J.

Gregory and I started dating soon after I arrived at Sweet Home. He was so polite and even opened the doors for me. He was special. He was always very conscientious and respectful. He loved his parents and was a good person. Gregory was the youngest of five. I think I fell in love with him right away. Because I grew up in the church and was a Christian, I would always tell myself that all Gregory lacked was a relationship with God. Other than that, I thought he was perfect.

As I mentioned, I was brought up in the church and came to know God as my personal Savior very early in life. My first encounter with God, whom I so fondly refer to as "the Big Guy," was at the age of five. I attended a large neighborhood elementary school, Griffen Memorial, where I would walk there and back. There were no buses. Either my mom or my grandmother would watch me go off to school each morning. The school was not very far, just a couple of blocks. This school always smelled funny, and I remember it always being too warm. This, however, is where I started my education.

The students at Griffen were very poor and seemingly did not have much. Sometimes the students would come to school without a coat in the winter. Often, I noticed that these students did not have the proper shoes either. I, on the other hand, always had what I needed. Perhaps this is why I started to feel a need to help people. Wanting to help was most likely a spillover from my days listening to my mom being called by her first name by the two Jewish ladies.

While I could not do anything about the clothes the students lacked, I could befriend them. This is what I did. I learned to play various sports from these children. I learned to play sports like kickball, dodgeball, and even double Dutch. Growing up, I played three things when not playing a sport: school, hospital, or church. My character role was that of the teacher, the doctor, or the missionary. My roles never changed. These were constants. When I was very young, I wanted to be a physician, most likely because I wanted to help people.

Although I was willing to befriend several of the students at school, many of the other students did not like me as much. I was not sure why, but I could always sense that I was more tolerated than asked to be someone's best friend. As I recall, I did not have a best friend until tenth grade. Because I was not a part of the group or the crowd, I was usually harassed. A large part of the harassment was the incidence of being picked out to be beat up after school. I considered myself to be a peacemaker. I didn't look for trouble, I looked for resolutions. Although I was shy and didn't have a gift of gab, I did have great reasoning ability, or so I thought. Once I found out the proposed outcome for the end of my school day, I attempted to deescalate the anticipated actions of the kids, by making small talk about absolutely nothing. This was just my way of trying to fit a circle into a square. This was my way of trying to divert the inevitable.

Growing up in the church taught me to turn the other cheek. I did not fully understand what that meant at five, but I thought I did. My dad always told us not to come home beat up but to turn the other cheek. Confusing at best. I grew tired of always being threatened and needing help. I was not sure who would help me. I was not sure where to even go for help.

From being in my Sunday school class, taught by my mom, I learned that God was able and willing to help His people. I was taught that God was always nearby for those who called Him and that he was a God who answered prayers. I believed that I was one of His people, so surely, He would help me. He did.

One very cold and gloomy day just prior to dismissal, I was given the all-too-familiar sign, the balled-up fist, which indicated I was going to be beaten up. I was so tired of this, so I decided to ask the Big Guy to help me. I did not really know the proper way to pray, but I knew how to say, "Help me, please." I heard the Lord tell me that He would walk me home and not to worry. I was not sure if I was telling myself this because I was so afraid or if it was possible that God himself was talking to me. I was very familiar with some of the Bible stories. I was very moved by how God was able to do so many things. I remembered the Red Sea story. I remembered the Wall of Jericho accounting. I remembered the story of Jonah. Most of all, I remembered the story of how God loved little children. Growing up, we all had the small, hard-covered Bibles with Jesus and the little lamb on the cover. How content this lamb seemed because Jesus was holding her! I was praying and believing that he would hold me, just like He was holding the lamb.

I left school that day not knowing what to think. I was looking for the Lord to come and walk me home. I know that I had never seen Him so how was this supposed to happen, I thought? As I lined up in the hallway outside my classroom to prepare to exit the building, I felt a little nervous because I did not see God. Where was He? Again, I thought, "Did I make this up? Did God really speak to me, a five-year-old? Was I just dreaming?" I did not know the story about the spies and the giants at this time, but the report was that there were several children waiting for me outside. When I got outside, I noticed these children. I remember how big they looked to me. They were like giants! I was so afraid. As I continued to walk ahead, I noticed that my right hand began to swing in a constant pendulous motion. I tried to stop the action, but I was not able to. The closer I got to the crowd of would be bullies, my hand continued to swing. I for whatever reason, no longer felt afraid. I no longer saw these children as giants. I could hear them yelling out things, but I did not hear them clearly. I felt such a peace. I felt so comforted. Yet, I was still looking for God. Where was He? When was He coming? How would I know when He arrived? What would He look like?

Just as in the story of the Red Sea, when the water receded, the children separated on either side of my path. The yelling continued, and my hand continued to swing in a pendulous motion, but there was no sight of God. The one pictured in the Bible story book.

Passing the crowd, I remember not feeling any fear. I was almost home. I was past the troubled times. When I got just about home, I once again heard the voice of God. I heard the Lord say to me, "I told you I would walk you home," and He did. Since that personal encounter with God, I have learned to trust Him even though I cannot see Him. I learned to believe in His voice. I learned to understand that I would always be able to trust God, even if I did not understand how things were going to work out.

All I wanted from this time on was to be liberated from the isolation, desolation, and depression I was feeling being at home with my mom. My move to Buffalo to help take care of my nieces was the answer to my prayer. It was going to take all that I learned from being walked home from school by Jesus, from turning the other cheek, and from learning at an early age how to trust and depend on God. I was building my own chapters for the 67th Book of the Bible. I, too, had a story to tell about the goodness of the Lord!

Moving in with my sister was much like the children of Israel transitioning to Canaan. My dad had been my Moses, helping to lead and guide me to a "better place." Just as with Moses and the children of Israel, he would not be going with me. The very thought of living with my sister, who was so loving, kind, and caring, was more than I could describe. Beverly lived in the suburbs. This was a big difference from living in the projects—in the inner city. I was on cloud nine. I was not sure how I was going to manage the care of Tamika and Leah, but I was sure going to do my best at becoming the nanny.

My two nieces were polar opposites. Leah was sweet and liked to hug. Tamika was challenging and loved to be disruptive. Leah had a passion for tea parties. She would often invite me and Beverly to her party. I did go, but I always wondered how she was able to fill her tiny plastic teacups with cold water. She was about three during this time. So being able to reach the facet and distinguish between the cold and hot sides was not something she could readily do. I remained skeptical. My sister, on the other hand, never gave the water temperature a thought. During a time that we graciously accepted an invitation to Leah's tea party, I asked her how she got the water so cold. She was quick to tell me that she got the water from the toilet! Needless to say, we didn't participate in a tea party for a long time.

Tamika was not as dainty. Both of them were smart. Both had amazing smiles. My nieces were beautiful. However, I would learn more about Tamika's character during this time. My sister lived in a duplex. We lived on the left side of the duplex. There was a common door to the entry that separated the units. This common area outside the entrance to the separate units is where Tamika noticed a ladybug. She was so fascinated by the creature that she tried to pet the bug. She then proceeded to pick up the ladybug and hold it in her hand for closer inspection. The wonderment in her eye was so interesting to me. I was holding fast to this little girl, appreciating the simplest things in life. I never remember having that experience. I began to live vicariously through what she was experiencing. I was at such peace, a peace that I really had never experienced before in a home environment. But then it happened so unexpectedly. Tamika dropped the ladybug on the ground and stomped on it! Devastated, I asked her, "Why would you do that?" She quickly, and without any sign of remorse, replied that she was tired of it, turned, and went inside the house. That experience of peace I had once been feeling left me immediately. I was now wondering if my original thoughts of the grass being greener on the other side were now a revelation that I was on turf.

As the days went on, I continued to settle into my new environment. However, I was watching carefully so I would not have my emotions held hostage. I began to set up my room, which consisted of a small dresser and a brown sofa bed in front of the only window in the room. The walls had two abstract pictures. I didn't like them, but they were part of the décor. All three bedrooms were upstairs, and one full bathroom was there too. I was comfortable. Downstairs were the living room, kitchen, dining room, and a half bathroom. Off of the kitchen was the back door, which led to a large grassy backyard devoid of any trees or shrubs.

After settling in and getting acclimated to my new surroundings, my sister registered me for school. I remember there were very few children in the neighborhood, but the neighborhood was diverse. I was determined to make as many friends as I could, quickly. I did just that. My first friend on my new street in my new town was Judy. We were the same age, and we found out that we had enough in common to hang out. After meeting Judy, I met her brother and sister, Mark and Holly. They, too, were very kind. Mark was rather standoffish only because he was very much into his music. He played the saxophone. Holly was wonderful and sweet and had hopes of running track in the Olympics. Bike riding was our favorite pastime. I learned to ride my 10-speed bike without hands. I learned this from Judy. So, things were different here than in the projects. I no longer felt the isolation once I realized growing up in the projects in my room. I was making new friends at my new home and in my new school. The Lord, who had in past years walked me home, was once again really present in my life.

I had always believed that God would give me the desires of my heart. I believed that God wanted me to be happy. I still believe in those things. At fifteen, I thought my natural happiness would begin with a life with Gregory. I was not initially attracted to him because he was not what I had always dreamed of when isolated in my room in Albany. But, as time went on, I learned more about him. Yes, he was an athlete, but he was also popular, and more importantly, he was smart.

As the days went on, I learned more about Greg and more about his personality. Describing Greg as jovial was an understatement. He was the life of the party and the voice of reason at the same time. The students looked up to him and had respect for him. The administrators of our high school also had great regard for Greg. He was gregarious. He was influential.

My sister became instantly enamored with Greg when she first met him. After all, he was polite and from a "good" family. He knew how to behave. This was a good thing. Soon after this, Gregory and I started to officially date. Our official first date would include going to the movies. I had never been to the movies, ever! This, too, was considered a sin. I think that because my sister was so wonderful, and had a great relationship with my mother, she convinced my mom to allow me to go to the movies with Greg. Living with Beverly was a blessing. A breath of fresh air.

I was so excited just to be going to the movies. I had no idea what to expect, but I was excited for whatever I would encounter. The fresh smell of popcorn and all the candy choices, combined with so many people, was, for me, like being in another world. All I could think was, "What else have I missed in my youth? What else had I not been privy to because of the beliefs of the church?" We were taught that going to the movies was a sin because "those people are there." Of course, I asked my mom, "What people?" Never getting an answer, I began to ask her if these were the same people that were going to the grocery store, going to the mall, and everywhere else we went to when not in church. No response.

Once we were finally seated in the theater, a heavy red-velvet curtain began to recede revealing the large white movie screen. Being in awe of the cold never explained how I was feeling. My encounter was much more. Once the sound engulfed the room and the lights went off, the roar of the MGM lion was equally impressive. I really wish I could remember the name of the film we watched, but I don't. The night ended well and I returned home before curfew. I will never forget that experience, just the name of the movie.

We were like no other couple I knew. Other couples were quite risqué. Many would sneak into bars, drink, and stay out late just partying and smoking weed. Greg and I were often poked fun at and referred to as the "old "couple. Our dates consisted mostly of going to the movies (I went to my very first one with him at sixteen) and going out to dinner. That's basically all we did. For eight months after we started dating, Gregory never initiated any sexual acts whatsoever. Yes, we kissed, but that really was it. I was starting to think that perhaps he was gay and just simply enjoyed my company. I told my best friend Kim, who introduced us, of my perceptions. She told me that I was wrong and that Greg was not gay, but he was a very nice guy. Greg and I continued to date, and he became more wonderful each day. I went to all his basketball games. He picked me up for every one of them. He would arrive with his two best friends, Darryl and Derrick, the twins. When Greg arrived at my house to pick me up, he would always come to the door and get me. If Beverly was home, he would always acknowledge her.

Whether it was Darryl or Derrick who were seated in the front seat of Greg's car, when I got to the car, whichever one it was in the front would relinquish the seat. Greg made sure that everyone treated me like a queen, just as he did. I learned that having a conversation with Greg before the games was not going to happen. It would ruin his concentration. The rides to school with the four of us were extremely quiet. There was very little, if any, talking. The rides home was exactly the same if Sweet Home lost the game.

While our relationship was going very well, I decided to allow the relationship to take a very dangerous and unnecessary turn. I turned from God by ignoring what He had told me earlier, specifically that I could have both Him and Greg. Although I fully understood what

God meant, I had a Hagar moment and decided that I knew the plans I should have for myself. I had these plans because I could not focus on what the Lord had said but only on what my emotions were dictating to me. Simply put, I was toying with becoming disobedient. Nor did I want to lose who I considered to be my Prince Charming. In spite of this, God still loved me. God has yet to look out for me. God continued to be good to me. God even continued to make me feel special, just as a dad would.

Scriptural Response

PSALM 37:4 (NRSV)

Take delight in the Lord; and He will give you the desires of your heart.

We Christians make a habit of limiting God. We piously declare that God provides for our needs, and we shouldn't beg God for anything more or above. We convince ourselves that we must be satisfied with what we have, and we should not honestly tell God what is on our hearts.

There are three scriptures that I share with my congregation often. I do this to remind them of God's character and God's love for us all.

(1) And my God will fully satisfy every need of yours according to His riches in glory in Christ Jesus. Of course, Paul was thanking the church in Philippi for their generosity to the saints, but he was also assuring them that God would not forget them and that God would provide for them as well. And so do we, too. God will supply all our needs, both spiritual and temporal. God gives to us lavishly; we have opportunities to give to others in need. God then gives to us when we have a need so that that need is satisfied. That's how God works—always looking out for us.

(2) The Lord is my Shepherd, I shall not want. (Psalm 23:1) Nothing new here; or is there? We recite this from memory as mere words, but if we take time to reflect and unpack this poetic presentation, we will find a gold mine of meaning.

It would take volumes to fully explain the metaphor of Jesus as a shepherd, but just allow me a little liberty to explain partially. The job of a shepherd was considered to be one of those jobs that no one revered. A first-century Palestinian shepherd was considered to be the scrub of the earth. They were dirty, isolated, and smelly. Their closest companions were sheep and other shepherds. The sheep were totally dependent on the shepherd for everything they would need for daily living. Since these sheep were raised for their wool and not for food, they lived long lives, and strong bonds were established between the shepherd and the sheep.

The shepherd protected them, fed them, watered them, cared for them, and bedded them down at night in pens of safety. If necessary, the shepherd would put himself in harm's way to protect the sheep. He was willing to die for them.

The shepherd-sheep relationship is one of love and trust. God loves us, and we need to trust God enough for God to provide all our wants.

(3) Take delight in the Lord, and He will give you the desires of your heart. I believe the psalmist is telling us to get happy learning about God, about God's word, about God's people, God's creation, and God's love. When we do, we are literally filled with the knowledge of God's being, in the world and in our lives. When this happens, we will not have time for frivolity or foolishness; we will concentrate on the things that please God and, thus, build us up.

Becoming God-minded puts us on a trajectory to experience and receive abundance from God. As James reminds us, we are going to ask of the Lord, but we are not going to ask amiss. Our hearts will be pure, and God will give the desires of our hearts.

In many ways, we can have it all; but our motives and our priorities must be in order.

Chapter Three
Prince Charming

Because of my upbringing, I would remain faithful to God by not defiling the Temple. I would not sleep with Gregory because I knew this was a sin. I did not want to sin. Shortly after we started dating, I once again heard the voice of God telling me that I could have Him and Greg. It was very clear to me that God was trying to convey to me that I should not feel pressured into having premarital sex. I believe that God gave His stamp of approval to the relationship I was developing with Greg.

Greg was everything to me and more. There was no reason to walk away from God. What I had learned as a child was that either you bring someone to your side or you follow them. I was not doing a good job bringing Greg to Christ. Now, he knew I was a "church girl," and I thought that was why he had increased interest in me and in our relationship. I had fallen into the enemy's trap. I was entangled with the lust of the flesh, the lust of the eye, and the pride of life.

My sister's newly acquired freedom gave her a new perspective on life. She once again could spread her wings and do something for herself. She was divorced and had the privilege of an in-home, unpaid nanny for her two girls. She was also the church organist, the best in town, and she would often play for more than one church when she could. Greg often picked up the slack for Beverly's responsibilities and helped "look after" me and the girls.

It was not uncommon for Beverly to stay away from the house for most of the day. Beverly was a sixth grade teacher and sat on many committees. Where we lived was a considerable distance from the city of Buffalo. Buffalo was where all the meetings, choir rehearsals, work, and socialization took place for Beverly. So, once the time grew late, Beverly would opt not to come home! Remember, I'm a city dweller, and the sounds and darkness of the suburbs were new to me. I loved everything about the place in the daytime, but when night fell, that was a different story. I was afraid. I was no longer in the confines of my bedroom; I was now living in an entire house with many rooms, all of which I was now responsible for.

Greg would almost always come by our house, with the approval of Beverly, after basketball practice. First, he would go home to shower, then make his way down the street, about two miles, to my house. I was always anxious, most of the time. Anxious about nightfall and putting the girls to bed, only to have the house quiet and strange sounds outside the house. My anxiety would soon turn into paranoia. Greg sensed this and would volunteer to stay with me until my sister returned home from the city. I was what my friends would call happy-sad, about this arrangement. I was happy because I was not alone and sad because I felt as though I was putting Greg out. After all, he had homework to finish, and should be home with his family, not babysitting me.

I would patiently await a call from Beverly, telling me that she would soon be on her way home. More often than not, that call would render me disappointed. The call ended with, "I'm not coming home tonight; I'm staying at Samantha's." Hysterics soon set in. I knew Greg was not able to stay with me; he had rules he had to adhere to from his parents as well. But stay, he did.

These incidents of my sister not coming home as promised became more frequent as time went on. Greg staying with me also became just as frequent. I was grateful for him staying, but now another problem would ensue. I would await Beverly's return by dinner time. I had served SpaghettiOs and grilled cheese sandwiches for days straight for lunch. However, I didn't know how to make dinner.

I would call Greg on these occasions. I was now despondent. I didn't have money for delivery, nor did I have a car, and even if I did, I did not have a license. Gregory would once again come to the rescue. Not only did he pick the three of us up, but he would also take us to Burger King or McDonald's to get dinner for me and the girls. I added the terms noble, gallant, and chivalrous to Greg's already impressive list of characteristics.

My initial idea of who Greg was had taken a 180-degree turn. Yes, he was amazing, yes, he was more than just an athlete and good student (who knew more vocabulary words than I did); he was wonderful and caring.

As wonderful and caring as Greg was, he lacked knowing and serving God. He did go to church on occasion, but he never mentioned giving his life to Christ, or being a born-again believer. I would have found him to be my ideal man, if only he knew God. He cursed like a sailor when other people upset him; he would fight whenever necessary, but he was never that way around me or the girls. I loved him, and the girls loved him.

I invited Greg to church with me on several occasions. I, of course, was more interested in showing him off to the other girls at church than discipling him to Christ, which should have been my first concern. I found myself getting further and further away from my relationship with the Lord. I was feeling torn and had convicted feelings, but I continued to dismiss those feelings in lieu of how I felt for Greg. The result? I got pregnant.

Scriptural Response

PSALM 119:11-16 (NKJV)

Your word I have hidden in my heart,
That I might not sin against You.
[12] Blessed are You, O LORD!
Teach me Your statutes.
[13] With my lips I have declared
All the judgments of Your mouth.
[14] I have rejoiced in the way of Your testimonies,
As much as in all riches.
[15] I will meditate on Your precepts,
And [a]contemplate Your ways.
[16] I will delight myself in Your statutes;
I will not forget Your word.

JERIMIAH 31:33

"This is the brand-new covenant that I will make with Israel when the time comes. I will put my law within them—write it on their hearts!—and be their God. And they will be my people. They will no longer go around setting up schools to teach each other about GOD. They'll know me firsthand, the dull and the bright, the smart and the slow. I'll wipe the slate clean for each of them. I'll forget they ever sinned!" GOD's Decree.

HEBREWS 8:10 (ESV)

For this is the covenant that I will make with the house of Israel
after those days, declares the Lord:
I will put my laws into their minds,
and write them on their hearts,
and I will be their God,
and they shall be my people.

Often times, we know the right thing to do because the right thing has been ingrained in us since our youth. The problem is not that we do not know, but rather that we do not hold on to the teachings and statutes of what we were taught. Why? Because seemingly something better comes along, and it may look more glamorous. The Bible speaks of "our foolish pride comes from this world, and so do our selfish desires and our desire to have everything we see. None of this comes from the Father," (1 John 2:16 CEV). So, with this, I in essence was falling off the wagon of Spiritual sobriety. I was not following the plan. The plan of salvation.

When we take our eyes off the LORD, and attempt to go our own way, we will fail. Success is not possible. God has previously written his law to us; now, in this new age, he has placed the laws in our hearts. The importance of this is the avoidance of sin. I missed the mark and felt horrific. I needed to get back on track. Even though I knew I had failed to represent Christ in the best way possible, I knew He yet loved me and would help me get back on track.

While these were the scriptures I used to understand my faults, I continued to repent and seek God for the forgiveness I needed. Falling down is not nearly as bad as not getting up. If you have fallen, get up!

Chapter Four

Detours and Determination

I graduated one year early from high school. This would turn out to be a really great thing for me. I was to be a part of the unofficial class of the bicentennial year, 1976. I would, however, have to wait until the following year to march with my class. Since I finished school a year early, I theoretically graduated the same year as Gregory.

I graduated early because I was asked to leave school. In the state of New York, eighteen credits were required for a Regents Diploma. From my time at Milne, I had accumulated extra credits that would be applied to my overall number of credits. My new high school in Amherst realized I had an excess of credits. By the time I completed the eleventh grade, I had a grand total of twenty-four credits! Having my butt in the seat at school would not provide any federal funding; therefore, I would need to leave. I was short a half credit of English, which I was required to take during the summer.

I reacted like a crazed child. I did not want to leave school. I begged the administration to let me stay. I could either tutor other students, take elective classes, or take an advanced placement class. The answer to all three was a resounding no! There was no way I could stay. I had to go. I learned from growing up in church that the Lord makes a way of escape. For me, escape was not having to go to school pregnant.

Following Greg's graduation day, we did our typical thing. We went to dinner. Greg always took me to really great restaurants. I went to my first five-star restaurant with Greg. That was a very good evening for both of us. I was so very proud of him; after all, he was on his way to a great learning experience at Buffalo State College. Greg wanted to major in business administration. Greg's desire was to follow in the footsteps of his brother, Charles, and work in the human resources field and later apply to law school. Greg had done very well in high school. He was very motivated by competition. He always believed that if any student could do well, he could do better. Gregory was confident, sure, and very capable. All of this was great. I was in love with someone smart, handsome, capable, and motivated. How fortunate was I? Somehow, though, I was beginning to lose sight of my purpose in this life. I lost sight of my soul's desire to serve God to the fullest.

Greg was taking a class in high school called Business Law. It was in this class that he had the greatest success with his competitive nature. Eric, a fellow classmate of Greg's, was also a student in this class. Eric was a National Honor Society member. Eric's overall cumulative average was 4.2. Eric excelled in every class. Most students who participated in the same classes as Eric were certain that he would be the one with the highest grade for the current quarter as well as the upcoming quarters. Seeing Eric in one's class was a signal that the grading curves would be higher and that there would be no way to obtain an A. That grade was reserved for just him. Little did Eric know that Greg was going to be a student in his next class, Business Law.

The teacher, Mr. O'Malley, made a really big deal every time he recognized the student who had the highest grade for the quarter. The announcement was like hearing about the winner of the Miss America contest. The same suspense and the same dramatic presentation would be evident. This was a one-semester course. There were to be only two grades given, not the traditional four as in a full year course. The first grading period came, and Mr. O'Malley went through his same antics of making the announcement of the top grade-earner of the class. Although it could be assumed that the winner would be Eric, Mr. O'Malley went through with the big ordeal as if someone else might take the virtual trophy. Just as sure as the sun rises in the East and sets in the West, Eric's name was called. As Eric stood to be acknowledged by the class, there was no clapping, no cheers, and no acknowledgement whatsoever by the students. This announcement threw Greg into some sort of tailspin. He was never going to allow this to happen again. He was determined to never allow Eric to beat him out of experiencing the feeling of such a great reward of having the highest grade.

In order for Greg to receive the honor of having the highest-grade point average in Mr. O'Malley's Business Law class, he would really have to buckle down and study hard. After all, he had some very serious competition to contend with. From that moment on, Greg behaved differently. Some sort of metamorphosis was beginning to take place. It was at this time that I noticed how determined Greg was becoming and how strong-willed he could be as well. Seemingly nothing would prevent him from reaching this goal or any other goal he might have in mind.

Greg was responsible for doing many of the same chores as most teenagers his age, and he was very focused on getting them done on schedule. His dad was very particular about how things should be done, especially the care and cutting of the lawn. Most often, Greg expressed a differing opinion from his dad on how the lawn should be cut. For years, this was to be an ongoing non-verbal fight between the two of them.

Basketball was Greg's passion. He so wanted to be just like Dr. J. He would sit and watch the games on television while holding his basketball, and in his mind, he would emulate the very movements of this famous athlete. Greg tried out for the Varsity team in high school and was able to get a starting spot as a forward. While Greg was not the most talented of the players, he possessed qualities of fortitude, stamina, and commodore. These were very much appreciated qualities that were required by the head coach, Mr. Walko.

While doing all of the necessary things to maintain his position on the basketball team, Greg was also studying to beat the band to achieve the highest grade in his Business Law class. I cannot over emphasize how badly Greg was able to excel at everything he put his mind to and how confident he was in his ability to succeed. As the second half, also the final semester of Business Law was fast approaching, the grades of the final accumulations were soon to be announced. Once again, the class braced themselves to hear the announcement that the winner for this semester would be Eric yet again. When Mr. O'Malley entered the classroom with his usual quiet demeanor and non-descript facial appearance, no one really paid any attention to him because the same thing was most likely going to happen again. Eric would be announced as the student with the highest-grade point average; the class would care less and continue to have a feeling of inferiority due to this reality. On this, the last day of the class, Mr. O'Malley made the same ritualistic motions for the grandiose announcement. He stood up erect, cleared his throat, and looked toward Eric. Nothing inherently different occurred; everything was pretty much status quo.

Eric began to have his virtual thank-you speech in mind already. The class could tell from his smirky facial features that this was so. As the entire class talked among themselves, not one student noticed how confident Eric was behaving in the anticipation of accepting the notoriety of having the highest grade yet again. What Eric did not know, as he was now positioned in a half-stance, was that Mr. O'Malley was not calling his name! Just as Mr. O'Malley said, "And the student with the highest grade for the quarter is," Eric was now in a fully erect position, ready to move toward the front of the class to bow. Mr. O'Malley finished his statement by saying "Gregory Giles."

The entire class, who was previously oblivious to the announcement for which they were expecting to hear Eric's name, was now jumping to their feet, clapping exuberantly, and cheering from the depths of their souls. This announcement seemingly caused great pangs for Eric. Humiliation was an understatement. Devastation would more than adequately describe Eric's current condition. From that moment on, I knew from the look on Greg's face, that he sincerely believed that nothing would ever defeat him again. How ideal it was to have one more characteristic added to his portfolio. That characteristic was preserved, as shown by his determination to achieve the impossible. I so loved this. Greg's character continued to show through as time went on.

Even with pregnancy, Greg was still outstanding. I had no idea what I was going to do. I was entirely too young to be a mom. Greg and I had just graduated from high school. Our parents would soon be involved. But first, I had to reveal that I was pregnant. Finding out that I was pregnant was crazy. We didn't have sex regularly—actually, hardly ever. Even though I wanted to be a physician, an OB-GYN, I missed how fertilization worked.

We drove to a Planned Parenthood over twenty miles away from where we lived to secure a definitive diagnosis. I remember the place well. I felt from that time on that I was the biggest disappointment to God ever. I was so depressed. I had so many plans but being pregnant at seventeen just wasn't in the plan. A blood test was performed, as was an internal exam. The doctor came back with the results and the announcement that I was indeed pregnant.

The doctor was very straight-forward in his delivery of the news to me. Greg was sitting out in the waiting area. On our way to Planned Parenthood, we had a serious conversation. However, for the first half of the ride, there was complete silence. I was thinking the obvious, "What if?" What if I was pregnant? How was I going to deal with this? How could I afford a baby? Who was going to help me? Greg had just been accepted into college. There is no way I would do anything to jeopardize this opportunity. I wanted Greg to be successful. I had hopes for my own success.

Once we were able to talk, during our twenty-mile ride to Planned Parenthood, Greg started talking first. He assured me that whatever the outcome of the test and whatever I wanted to do, he would support my decision. The awesomeness of this young man continued to impress me. Now I was challenged with telling my mom. Greg told his parents first. I chose to tell my oldest sister, Harriet, and not my mother.

I went upstairs to the bathroom and sat on the bathroom floor. I dialed her number, holding my breath the entire time. I continued to hold my breath until she picked up the phone. "Hello," she said. I responded with a very quiet "hello." Then complete silence, until Harriet asked why I was calling so late. I didn't think it was late; it was only 10 o'clock p.m. I told her I had to tell her something. She said, "Go ahead." I remember just blurting out my news, "I'm three months pregnant."

"Okay," she said. That's it. No yelling at me. No condemnation. No statement of being disappointed—just a simple, okay. I was feeling loved. Harriet told me she would tell my mother and not to worry about anything.

Scriptural Response

JOHN 16:13 (ERV)

But when the Spirit of truth comes, he will lead you into all truth. He will not speak his own words. He will speak only what he hears and will tell you what will happen in the future.

A divine appointment is defined as an encounter that is believed to have been orchestrated by God. A major function of the Holy Spirit is to lead and guide us into all truth (John 16:13). Even when we are engulfed in our own thoughts and notions, He is there earnest to do His work in us. We can be so focused on so many good things, giving our best efforts to them, and still miss what God wants us to plainly see. Busy lives, as students, parents, and spouses often leave us with our heads turning. We must be careful to pay attention to our motives and actions. A good thing is not always the right thing!

The book of Acts 9:1-19 discusses the conversion of Saul, who was notorious for persecuting those who converted from Judaism to Christianity. In his mind, his notions led him to believe he was doing the right thing. He justified his actions by his own thoughts and beliefs. It wasn't until something dramatic and seemingly devastating happened to him (he fell blind) that he was introduced to a new thought. Now, in this blind state, God was able to harness his attention, speak to him, and share the Truth with him, forever changing his life and his ministry. The truth really does set us free (John 8:32).

When God shows you the truth about yourself or even someone in your life, do yourself a favor and believe him! It may not be comfortable or feel good at its first hearing, but the journey with Him is how the truth gets to work perfectly in us, changing us from the inside out. The Lord loves us. He wants what's best for us. He wants us to accept His truth and be free!

Chapter Five
Taking Charge

The pregnancy brought new issues. I was working full time at a department store as a salesclerk. I loved my job because I loved clothes and always considered myself to be a fashionista. Working this job allowed me to stay stylish, with a discount! This was the best job. I worked during the week and most Saturdays. As the pregnancy progressed, I noticed how tired I was becoming. Unlike most of the teenagers I worked with, I did not have to wait for a ride because I had my own car.

Along with my other noted characteristics, I felt I was a good negotiator. I was seventeen when I got pregnant and sixteen-and-a-half when I graduated from high school. My mom was still receiving child support from my dad. Considering where we lived and public transportation being nonexistent, having a car was a necessity. I was certainly not able to buy a car on a salesclerk salary. The hourly wage I received was not life sustaining and definitely would not support a car payment, making only the minimum wage.

An idea formed in my head, and I quickly acted. My mother was receiving one hundred ten dollars a month for child support. After doing a bit of research, I realized that I could get a new car with a monthly payment equal to my monthly child support. While I did not have a past history of fond conversations with my mom, I was prepared to go into negotiations with an expectant heart. My argument for asking her to relinquish the monthly support check was presented as a merger of funding for the acquisition of a vehicle. My speaking points were simple and basic. I reminded my mom of how fortunate I was to have a job that benefits not only my pocket but also provides a discount for clothes. My mom was keenly aware of how much I loved clothes. Secondly, while the job was only a few miles away from my sister's house, public transportation was not an option.

I threw out the possibility of taking cabs to and from work, just because I knew that was never going to go over well. So, even if my mom was already forming an opinion that would not be what I wanted to hear, mentioning being in a car with a strange person, a man, was certainly not going to be acceptable. My first two arguments were solid. Now I needed to provide the clincher for my argument. According to what is taught about debates and winning arguments, it is best to present a well-constructed counterargument rather than blatantly telling someone they are wrong. Thirdly, I mentioned to my mom how having a car would be helpful to Beverly. Beverly, after all, was my mom's favorite child. Beverly did nothing wrong. Beverly never gave my mom any backtalk and was the only child who agreed most with whatever my mom had to say. So, in my closing argument, I was sure to convey the most positive side of me having the funds from child support to pay for the car: helping Beverly.

My negotiation ability worked in my favor, and my dad would soon travel to Buffalo from Schenectady to purchase the car. My first car was red, shiny, and brand new. My dad came to town for a weekend and did all the paperwork to purchase the car. A 1976 Plymouth Arrow hatchback was my new ride. The caveat to this was that I did not yet have my driver's license. However, the hardest part was over, dealing with my mom and convincing her that this idea was best.

Having the car would now afford me even greater opportunities. While it is true that I loved my job as a salesperson and was excited about receiving discounts for clothes, this job would not sustain me and the needs of a new baby. My hopes of going to medical school were now certainly placed on hold. My entire educational career was incorporated with studies and electives to promote going to medical school. I have an amazing affinity for learning math and the natural sciences. Going to medical school and becoming a physician was my lifelong dream.

Quick thinking is what I was now faced with in order to support myself and the baby. Greg was very present and very helpful. He did not treat me any differently now that I was pregnant than before I learned that I was having a baby. Greg remained an all-around good guy. He was kind, sweet, and compassionate, just like always. I was raised to be self-sufficient. I needed to find a way to become just that: self-sufficient.

As the Lord often does, he provided information to come to me. In the mail was a postcard that advertised a new educational program. The program was a six-month computer programming course. Wait! I could have a career in only six months, before the expected birth and support my baby. This was too good to be true. I was enrolled in the program and despised every minute of the course work. I liked to talk too much to want to pursue a career of becoming best friends with a computer, punch cards, and sheets of green and white computer paper. Nothing about this scenario was close to being a physician and helping people recover from their health issues.

I completed the program and went back to work in retail. During this time, my sister was on her way back to work as a teacher. My oldest niece, Tamika, was going to be starting kindergarten, but Leah still needed a babysitter. My sister had no relationship with the neighbors, so she was not able to ask a neighbor about keeping Leah. Now what? Someone needed to provide care for Leah, especially since I was going back to work and Beverly was going back to work. Once again, I took the initiative of a grownup and went to work looking for daycare.

I put Leah in a stroller and began to walk the neighborhood, looking for a solution. Without having any direction or idea where to start, I took off on my journey with focus and determination. I set out to find someone trustworthy to watch baby Leah. Considering I was only seventeen and not totally sure what constituted trustworthiness in a person, especially someone I did not know, As I walked our street in search of the special person, I walked with purpose. I was going to master this task. After all, I embodied confidence, resiliency, and complete confidence in my abilities. I believed this because of my exceptional mastery of my educational journey. More than that, I remember my dad telling me from the time I was a little girl that I could do anything that I wanted to do, if I tried really hard. For me, this was profound, considering my father did not make it past the third grade and was illiterate.

In spite of that, to me, my dad was the most brilliant man I had ever known. For people who didn't know our family intimately, this information about my dad was not known. My dad owned two upholstery businesses. One in Albany and one in Schenectady, "Tucker's Upholstery." If you are wondering how my father was able to be successful and illiterate, it is important to know that he had a keen sense of direction, and I believe he possessed a photographic memory. Whenever he was called out to the home of a potential customer, carrying his massive sample books, intending to make a sale, he would have someone drive him.

On the drive, he would pay close attention to the streets, the landmarks, and the number of lights between each left or right turn. My dad was born in Lynchville, Virginia, and would often drive there and to Baltimore, Maryland, too. I asked my dad how he was able and comfortable to drive so far away from home without being able to read. After all, he could not count the number of lights before right and left turns, and the landmarks most probably became distorted due to the growth of the cities and new construction. His answer was simple and straight-forward. He told me he did pay attention to the large and more common landmarks as he traveled. He noticed particular trees that were consistent on his way. Noticing those landmarks and trees gave him confidence that he was on the right path to his destination.

Mesmerized by his response to me, I was moved to ask one more question. I asked my dad how he would know what to do in the event of a detour. Once again, he responded with such candor and simplicity; he said, "I follow the other people, and soon I would be back on track." He laughed as he answered me. This laugh was sort of like how I imagined Sarah laughing at the visiting angels when they came to tell her she was going to be a mother past the age of conception and Abraham, at ninety-nine years old, would become a father. In other words, I thought he was telling me I lacked faith in his ability to do things most people couldn't or would never believe they could do.

I was now three blocks away from our home, pushing Leah in her stroller, looking for just the right place to stop. I did not have anyone to follow. I did not have any familiar landmarks or, for that fact, any special trees to take note of on my quest to find my destination. The first few doors I approached, no one was home. Finally, I was in the middle of the third block, and Eureka, someone actually answered the door. A beautiful young Black woman with a short, well-manicured hair style, a beautiful smile, and a kind face. I remember introducing myself to her and explaining why this teenager, with a toddler in tow, was knocking on her door. "Hi, I'm Alicia, and this is my niece, Leah," I told her. She responded, "Hi, my name is Janice; nice to meet you," with her beautiful smile now transitioning to a look of wonderment. Again, my mind went back to scripture, and I imagined how Sarah's facial features might have transitioned from laughter to wonderment at the news of having a baby.

Janice invited us in, even before she knew the nature of our visit. Her home was neat, clean, and smelled nice. It was sort of like fresh linen before we learned how to bottle that smell as an air freshener. I was quick and forthright in explaining why I was there and what I was in search of. Once again, I went into negotiations. A skill I believed I was becoming quite good at doing. I made sure that I highlighted the most important feature of my negotiation. That was, how amazing, important, and stuck in a precarious situation my sister was challenged with.

I explained that my sister was a schoolteacher in Buffalo, and I graduated early from high school due to exceptional academic success, and we were both working full-time. I provided information about our living situation; Beverly was a divorced parent of two children, with a teenage sister (me) coming to help and no one to keep the baby. After presenting the most substantive component of my argument, I now wanted to present a plea for help.

I continued telling Janice that we have a wonderful family dynamic. Never once did I mention my pregnancy. I did not want Janice to feel sorry for our situation because we were pitiful, but rather I wanted to convince her how important her lending help to us would be. She was willing to help and committed to taking care of Leah. I planned for Beverly and Janice to meet with each other to work out the part of the negotiation I could not, such as how much she would be paid and the hours she would need to care for Leah. My mission was accomplished.

Scriptural Response

PROVERBS: 16:9

"In their hearts humans plan their course, but the Lord establishes their steps."

PROVERBS: 19:21

"Many are the plans in a person's heart, but it is the Lord's purpose that prevails."

PROVERBS: 20:24

"A man's steps are from the Lord; how then can man understand his way?" God allows us to use our skills and talents, but it is he who brings things to pass. We can do nothing apart from God. He must allow or permit our plans to happen.

LUKE: 5:5

"Simon answered, Master, we've worked hard all night and haven't caught anything. But because you say so, I will let down the nets. Simon Peter was a skilled, master fisherman. This was his profession, and he knew his fishing business very well. Despite his great skill, Jesus was the one to bring his plans for a catch to fruition.

JOSHUA 1:8 (New King James Version)

"This Book of the Law shall not depart from your mouth, but you shall meditate on it day and night, that you may observe to do according to all that is written in it. For then you will make your way prosperous, and then you will have good success."

We need the Lord in everything we do. It is he who gives us good success! Know that God is a loving God who wants you to give you good things; he wants you to prosper spiritually and naturally. We need to put our trust in him to make his plan prevail.

Chapter Six

The Birth

Greg's mom, who worked as a nurse, promised my mother she would help me secure a doctor so I could start my prenatal care and have a healthy baby. This decision was made soon after the "moms" had their talk. Greg's mom expressed how distraught she was, while my mother just kept complaining about why I chose to tell Harriet about the pregnancy before her. I am not sure why that was her biggest concern, but that was her focus. During the maternal conversations, there was a proposed decision for immediate marriage. This conversation and decision to marry were held without the voice or opinion of the new parents to be, me and Greg.

Greg and I were adamant about not getting married. Greg was in his first year of college, and I was still working retail, trying to figure out my life. What I did know was that I did not want to be married. I had enough to contend with in accepting the fact that I was going to be a mother. No way was I equipped to be both a mother and a wife. Greg and I had distinct reasons why we should not marry. Besides being too young, I was adamant about not being a mom on welfare.

Not that I was any less concerned about the pursuit of my life goals, but I was more concerned about Greg's goals and the importance of achieving his educational goals. At seventeen and nineteen, we both knew it would be far more advantageous for Greg to complete school than to go to work at a plant and get married. The skills I was utilizing now were more specific to comparative analysis than negotiating. The very thought of Greg leaving school in his first year was unconscionable. I could not stop thinking about what would happen to us if he was laid off from the plant (he would have been low on the seniority list), and the only position he could find was at a fast-food joint. Umm, this was not the life I was looking for, nor was it the life I could contend with. I liked nice things. I wanted to have nice things. The option of ending up at a local fast-food establishment was not doable.

Greg's mom never secured the OB/GYN doctor for me, so once again, Alicia was required to come to her own rescue. I learned to be self-sufficient early in life. I most likely acquired this characteristic during middle school, when I was able to do modules to keep busy. By the way, this is what led to my having excess credits and graduating early. I was three months pregnant when I was examined at Planned Parenthood. I was three months pregnant, and I envisioned that the baby was already well on his way to looking more like a human than a fetus. I remember the doctor telling me that he could hear the heartbeat, but I could still make the decision today to terminate the baby. I became irritated and angry with the doctor. How was I going to kill my baby—our baby?

Time, in my mind, was of the essence. I needed to take care of my baby now! I hung out with my best friend Kim often because she was always helpful and in my corner. We had grown very close in the years we were together in high school. We often hung out after school and watched movies at her house. Her mom and my sister, Beverly, worked together at the same elementary school. We were like family. The day I decided to take matters into my own hands, I happened to be at Kim's house.

I asked Kim for her Yellow Page phone book because I needed to look up the 1-800 number for the American Medical Association (AMA). I called the AMA while sitting on the bed in Kim's mom's room. I explained to the lady who was assisting me that I was a teenager and I was looking for a physician who was experienced with teen pregnancies. Five physician referrals were provided to me. I called the first doctor on the list. I was given an appointment for the next week. I was so thankful for my car. I was able to take myself to places I needed to be without having to rely on other people to get me there. I was feeling more independent and more like a functioning adult in a child's body, carrying a child.

During my first visit to my new doctor, I was examined and told my predicted due date. I remember my new doctor being very soft-spoken, very kind, and not condescending. He did not make me feel as though I was a nobody, but rather he was rather fatherly. He talked to me about the importance of taking my prenatal vitamins and how important it was for the baby's well-being. Up to my seventh month, my pregnancy was going well.

By the time I reached my seventh month, the start of my third trimester, I began having trouble with my blood pressure. Up until this point, my blood pressure would fluctuate between normal and borderline high. I was experiencing consistent high blood pressure issues. I was diagnosed as having pre-eclampsia. At first, we tried the medication phenobarbital to help control my blood pressure, and I was told not to eat excessive salt and to rest. I was accustomed to being obedient, and this was not a time to change my ways. As hard as it was, I didn't eat potato chips. I loved to eat potato chips. What kid didn't?

I would not make it to full term. Even with medication, rest, and no added salt to my diet, I was still experiencing high blood pressure. The only alternative now was to be admitted to the hospital for extensive rest and constant observation. During my admission to the hospital, Kim remained a true friend. She visited with me every day. I loved her for this. I was becoming more afraid as the days went on. My blood pressure was not going down as much as the doctor would have liked. I was told to lie on my left side for most of the day to increase blood flow and oxygenation for my baby. I was compliant. I wanted a healthy baby. Being compliant made me a good mother. I wanted to be the best mother, not just a good mother.

The next morning, day three of my hospital stay, I continued with the same ritual as always. My weight was taken before I could eat. I was not going to have breakfast that day because I was going to have my labor induced and have the baby. This was important because my pressure was now at an alarming level. A level not compatible with life. As soon as my mother heard of my hospitalization, she quickly came to Buffalo to be with me.

Once the induction started, once the pitocin was hung, I just laid there hungry and afraid, waiting for the first induced contraction. The room was very solemn. My mother, my sister Beverly, and Kim were present with me. Greg was at work. He always worked in the plant during the summer to save for tuition for the upcoming semester. My brother-in-law was instrumental in helping to locate Greg and making him aware that it was time to come to the hospital. His baby was on the way.

I was indeed happy that Greg was soon on his way. Finally, the contractions were becoming more intense. This was to be a natural childbirth because of the amount of medication I was already receiving in an attempt to control my blood pressure. However, my pressure remained dangerously high during labor. Beverly was my angel of the day. She held my hand and spoke softly to me during each contraction. Each god-awful pitocin-induced contraction. Greg arrived. He looked so sad. I was the only one in the room who did not look so sad. I was just in intense pain.

I remember that Greg sat at a distance from me. He had a look of concern, but also a look of fear. I was not able to decipher the mood of the room, but I knew something was different. This was not how it looked on television when a mom was about to give birth. On television, everyone seemed happy and hopeful, with great anticipation. The people in my room looked as if they were attending a funeral. I had now been in labor for six hours. I was growing tired of hearing "You Light Up My Life" played over and over. This was the popular song sung by Debbie Boone, and I wanted to go to delivery just so I could stop hearing this song.

My doctor finally came into my room. He addressed all those present and then announced that I was going into delivery. It was time. My doctor asked my mom to accompany me to the delivery. That was the most confusing time of the entire day. Delivery did not take long. Soon, I gave birth to a sweet, beautiful baby boy weighing four pounds and eight ounces. Soon after delivery and recovery, I was escorted back to my room. Once I entered my room, all I could see, spread out all over the bed, was a birth-to-one year layette. A menagerie of clothing was sent to baby Greg by my sister, Harriet. How blessed was this baby? It would be days later that I discovered the reason for the solemnity during my labor. My doctor informed my family that I most likely would not live through childbirth, and he wanted to prepare them all for my possible demise. But God!

Scriptural Response

ISAIAH 40:29

"He gives power to the faint, and to him who has no might, he increases strength.'

Life's circumstances aren't always pleasant or easy to go through. Even with our best intentions to be hopeful and full of faith, we must understand that preparing for something is totally different from experiencing it.

Doing my due diligence to be as ready as possible to give birth to my son, the process of labor was daunting and tiring. God knew all along what he was going to do in the delivery room. The right doctor, the right people around me, and the right hope within me—God was there. He brought both mom and baby through a tough situation.

2 Corinthians 12:9 "And He said to me, "My grace is sufficient for you, for My strength is made perfect in weakness...""

When we feel our lowest, the most tired and ready to faint, God is strong in us. He equips us with his strength to endure, to see a thing through to the end.

John 16:21 "When a woman is giving birth, she has sorrow because her hour has come, but when she has delivered the baby, she no longer remembers the anguish but the joy that a human being has been born into the world."

The gift of childbirth is such an amazing, rewarding, painful, and emotional happening. No one experiences the woes and joys quite like the expecting mother. She is alone in her predicament. Oftentimes, when the rubber meets the proverbial "road", we are standing alone. Even with a circle of support, you can feel, even utterly alone. That is when we must believe that the God of all providence and grace will not only give us the blessed end result, but also the strength to get through it.

Chapter Seven

Jumping the Broom

By 1981, I was finally married. I was almost twenty-two years old. We had braved the birth of our first child out of wedlock, now four years old, celebrated Greg's graduation from college, and were looking forward to the expectations of a great future. When Greg and I married, we lived in a two-bedroom apartment with our son, Little Greg. Greg had secured a position as a claims adjuster with a well-known insurance company. I also worked as a respiratory therapist in a local two-hundred-bed hospital. Life as we knew it was excellent, and the expectations for the future seemed very promising.

Ever since I bore Greg a son, his first and only child, he was totally committed to being responsible for little Greg's well-being. Greg provided child support every week without the instruction or cohesion of any court system. For Gregory, providing support was his duty and his pleasure. Greg's family was equally supportive of their efforts in helping care for the well-being of our son.

When I was told by God (the Big Guy) at sixteen that I could have He and Greg for whatever reasons, I could not hold on to this and trust God completely. I decided to have a Sari experience and create some means to put an end to this promise. I entered into an Ishmael experience. By that, I mean I did not wait on God but took matters into my own hands by electing to make sense of something I did not understand.

I was the one who decided that, because God made this grandiose statement to me, whatever would happen would be in His will. I later discovered the difference between God's perfect and permissive will. I was existing in God's permissive will. I would later understand that this was not the best place to be. Due to this fact, when attempting to conceive another child to help celebrate our marriage, which proved unsuccessful, I immediately felt that God was punishing me for something. That something in my mind was conceiving a child out of wedlock. It was not until years later that I learned this was not the motive of God. God behaves lovingly towards us, not vindictively as we do. I mixed Him up with the way we are when others mistreat us. I failed to understand that God is love, and love does not misbehave.

Following six years of trying to conceive, Greg and I were finally expecting the birth of our second child in the fall of 1986. We tried and investigated almost every method to enhance the possibility of conceiving as much as possible. We went to the doctor and spent much of our money to get pregnant. I began to read one book after another until the reading totaled volumes of books loaded with information on the science of conception.

My gynecologist was not overly helpful or very enthusiastic about helping us. His thought was simple: he believed that because I had one child without difficulty, having another pregnancy should be of no consequence. My doctor, as I soon discovered, could not be further from the truth. In my reading, I was most likely ovulating way too early in my cycle. I would need some medical intervention to conceive. I tried to explain the findings to my doctor regarding the information I obtained in my research from reading. Dr. Achar was not going to go along with this at all. He held on to his conviction that because I already had one child, having another should not be a problem. Dr. Achar would soon discover that this line of thinking would quickly be discredited by what I found in the literature.

Little Greg (fondly called Greg M) was now eight years old and the proud owner of a science microscope set. This was a gift he most likely received for his birthday or Christmas. From my literary research, I better understood how the female cycle operated and the conditions necessary to make conception possible. Once ovulation occurred, the pattern within the cervical secretions changed to a more telltale sign indicating that ovulation had occurred. With this newfound information, I retrieved a sample of my cervical secretions. I placed the smear on the microscope slide of my son's science kit. Having taken several science classes in undergraduate coursework, I also knew how to affix a slide cover over the obtained specimen to maintain the stability of the sample.

When I went to the doctor that same day for another infertility check-up, although the doctor stated I was okay and should not be classified as infertile, I took along with me this prepared slide. When I got to the examination room and immediately after Dr. Achar walked in, I asked him if he had a microscope. He looked puzzled by my line of questioning and asked me what I had done. I again questioned him about the availability of a microscope on the premises and the need for him to look at something. For six months before this time, I had been trying to obtain a script for Clomid. This fertility drug has an indication for improving conception rates. Every time I asked Dr. Achar for the prescription, I was refused the medication simply because Dr. Achar sincerely believed that I did not need this line of intervention to be able to conceive.

Once I handed Dr. Achar my at-home, makeshift laboratory-prepared slide, he immediately took it away to look at its contents. Within less than two minutes, Dr. Achar, who left the exam room with only one item in his hand, was back with two things. The first was the slide I gave him, and the second was a prescription for Clomid. I had indeed been ovulating too early in the cycle. This definitely decreased my chances of conception. I was pregnant three months later after getting my script. I delivered a healthy seven-pound, ten-pound baby boy, Austin Kyle, whom Greg and I called our Clomid baby. Austin was my second significant gift from God, and I loved him.

Before delivering Austin, I mentioned to Greg that I did not want to bring my new baby home to the apartment we were living in. Still, I tried to get him home to a house. Immediately, Greg went into action. He had the same dedication and commitment that I had seen with him in making the basketball team, obtaining the highest grade in business law, taking care of Little Greg without any pressure from anyone, graduating from college with a 3.5 total grade point average, and steadily functioning as a great father and wonderful husband.

Greg began his research of the Buffalo, New York, housing market and became very knowledgeable. Greg did what he did best; he took care of me and all of my needs. In this respect, he was just like the Big Guy; he was excited about giving me the desires of my heart.

We did indeed purchase our first home, and I did love it. Not because the house was big or in a prestigious neighborhood, but because that was not the case. The house was situated in a small community on a major thoroughfare between the cities of Buffalo and Niagara Falls, New York, in a hamlet called the Town of Tonawanda. The Town of Tonawanda was a comfortably mixed neighborhood, allowing residents to participate in diversity. The schools were highly recommended, and the taxes were more than reasonable. This was a lovely place to live and raise a family. Yet again, Greg had brought happiness to me and the family. We moved into our new house on Niagara Falls Boulevard and began the next phase of our lives.

My desire to work until the very last moment was at the forefront of my mind. I wanted to continue to help support my family by working as long as possible before going out on maternity leave from the hospital. I was very fortunate to have such an excellent therapist to work with. We were just like family. Everyone supported each other and helped out whenever they could. This was incredibly wonderful because I was beginning to tire as I neared the latter stages of my second semester. I was starting to grow tired of the 13-hour night shifts because they went on forever. The therapist tried to assist me with my workload as much as possible. For this, I was very grateful and felt very fortunate and blessed again.

Around this time of my gestational period, about six and one-half months now, Greg and I wanted to ensure that nothing would change too drastically for little Greg, so we kept him on his schedule. This schedule included participating in his Boy Scout troop. We had already ventured past the soap car derby and the whittling experience. We were on to even more fun activities, the summertime picnic.

Having to work the night before the picnic, I could only catch a few hours of sleep before getting up to tag along with both big Greg and little Greg to the picnic. This had to be one of the hottest days, and I was overwhelmed. I was devastated due to the heat and the fatigue I was experiencing. Although little Greg had been in the scouts for some time, he was a Webelos. I was not very acquainted with many parents—only a few. I grew increasingly tired as I sat on the hard picnic bench under the pavilion reserved for us. I was polite to everyone but desired to go home and go back to sleep for about two days.

Soon after moving to our new dwelling place, my husband was sought out by the local political party to run on the Republican ticket for City Councilman for the Town of Tonawanda. Greg could always be found talking to people about anything and almost everything. Greg was well-rounded and could speak with everyone, regardless of who they were. Greg was very comfortable with his ability to do this.

He was not overly cocky; he was very confident and thought very highly of himself in this respect. Greg was very caviler and ambitious, and many people noticed this about him. People liked talking to Greg. People wanted to get to know him.

While we were at the picnic, a man, who we would later find out was named Bob, talked with Greg for over two hours about sports and other nonessential conversation materials unrelated to the Scouts. After giving Greg the sign for wanting to go home now and a very subtle nod towards the car's direction, he began to wrap up his conversation, and we headed home.

When we walked into the house, we noticed that the light on the answering machine was lit up, indicating that a message was waiting to be heard. As I did my best to meander up the stairs and go to bed, I heard Greg calling me to come back downstairs to listen to the message on the machine. In the short time it took us—fifteen minutes, to get home from the picnic sight, Bob had called Greg about a job opportunity.

We did not quite understand why Bob was so moved by the conversation he and Greg had at the picnic. While listening to the message on the phone answering machine, we listened to Bob elaborate on how impressed he was with Greg. We listened to how Bob expressed his belief in Greg's ability to obtain a position with one of the most prestigious pharmaceutical companies in the country. The purpose of the message and call was to encourage Greg to apply for a job with his company. The message was short and precise. While that was true, we played the message repeatedly, trying to make sure we heard the message correctly. As Greg and I looked at each other in disbelief, we attempted to get on with the rest of our day without discussing the meaning or purpose of Bob's message.

The following day, Bob called again. This time, he and Greg actually spoke. I could tell from Greg's facial expressions that he was becoming very interested in the content of the conversation. Bob had invited Greg to apply for a position as a pharmaceutical sales representative with his company. Greg conveyed to Bob that he was somewhat perplexed about this entire conversation but nonetheless honored that he would even be considered by Bob to work for his company.

Greg's current position was with a well-known insurance company, enabling us to have a comfortable lifestyle. This position allowed Greg to come and go as he pleased to take care of the business while driving a very up-to-date company car and maintaining an expense account. The most appealing part of Greg's position was that he worked from home, and his home office was over 200 miles away. Greg was an independent contractor, managing his affairs and doing this very well. While it was confirmed that Greg was happy and content with the insurance job, the lingering thought about the pharmaceutical experience was more appealing to him. The likelihood of pursuing a position with the pharmaceutical company was starting to infect his being. Soon, calls were coming in from the drug company's human resources department. This was now becoming a slippery slope adventure that Greg was beginning not to be able to avoid.

Greg talked with John, the HR representative, and the entire process was beginning. By the time six months had lapsed, Greg had been flown back and forth to Indiana, and by the time he had interviewed and convinced the CEO that even though he did not have a science background, he was able to do the job, Greg was offered a position with the company. For Greg to begin an appointment with this company, he must have an immediate physical. Because the offer came in at 8:30 in the evening, it would take a lot of work to locate a physician to perform a physical. However, because of my relationship with many people at my hospital, I could call on the husband of a close therapist friend, a physician, and ask him to do Greg's physical that night. Rob agreed to perform the physical and did so at his home. Following the completion of all the requirements, Greg started his new career.

After starting his new job, Greg first prioritized meeting with his sales manager. Greg was instructed to select the finest restaurant in our area, preferably a five-star establishment, would be apropos. Greg's sales manager came to our home, the house I was so proud of because it was my first, immediately stating that the place was inappropriate for the position he was newly hired for. I felt such a sense of disappointment. Why wasn't my house good enough? What was wrong with my home? I was feeling more than disappointed; I was feeling inadequate as well. The question I was fielding was how this man could come into my house and make such a declaration regarding my home. What gave him the right to determine this, and on what basis? I was not happy with this statement at all.

Despite my dissatisfaction, I tried not to let on to this at dinner. The restaurant was very exquisite and was, in fact, a five-star establishment. I was not overly impressed. This may have had something to do with the fact that I was still pondering why my house was not adequate.

Once the meal came, I was not impressed with the food after my fork had been switched out repeatedly. The whole green beans, which were very few in number, needed to be cooked longer for my taste. The beef was cooked adequately, and the potatoes were okay, but the best part of the meal for me was the sorbet, served between courses to clean the pallet for the next course. I had never been anywhere where that was included in ordinary events.

Approximately six months following the start of Greg's new position with the pharmaceutical company, we moved to a much bigger home in a relatively upscale and prestigious area. I felt somewhat out of place, but that feeling would not linger. I absolutely grew to love this house. I loved my home. This home had a separate dining room; I did not even have a dining room in my first house, a pool, four bedrooms, and a huge family room. The interior of the house was perfect. The wallpaper did not even need to be changed. Everything was just perfect. I felt grateful for Bill's comments about my first home because they helped me see the need to move up. Greg's job would bring with it quite a different appeal. Greg would be speaking to physicians and he would only be taken seriously if he had the correct address. As crass as this may seem, this is how it was during this period. Sure enough, almost every physician would inquire from Greg where it was that he resided.

The big house on the hill brought more significant problems than I could imagine. While I enjoyed the house and the part of town in which it was located, Williamsville, New York, this would be more than we needed.

Scriptural Response

"Delight yourself in the Lord, and he will give you the desires of your heart." Psalm 37:4 lets us know that we should delight in the presence, provision, and promise of God. We do this when we obey him, and his word, not our feelings, fears, or thoughts. God really is omniscient. He knows everything about us and our lives. We should trust and accept that truth over any other thought. It is then we can honestly say he is Lord of our lives.

GENESIS 2:23-24

"The man said, this is now bone of my bones and the flesh of my flesh; She shall be called Woman, because she was taken out of Man. For this reason, a man shall leave his father and his mother, and be joined to his wife; and they shall become one flesh.

MARK 10:6-12

"But from the beginning of creation, God made them male and female. For this reason, a man shall leave his father and mother, and the two shall become one flesh; so they are no longer two, but one flesh."

HEBREWS 13:4

Marriage is to be held in honor among all, and the marriage bed is to be undefiled; for fornicators and adulterers God will judge.

It is clear that God has designed sex for us, but within the confines of marriage. Man and woman are to be husband and wife. There are many scriptures that lay out the 'rules' about sex. All of them let us know that sex is a part of God's plan. His plan is designed to protect us from emotional hurt, physical disease, and psychological damage, all of which can happen when we take matters into our own hands and go outside the plan of God.

Sex is special, personal, intimate, bonding, and pleasurable. It's supposed to be. God has given man this special gift: within the confines of his covenant, marriage and sex are also safe, sanctified, and sacred. It is no less abominable to curse God's name, his person, or his character than it is to have sex outside of marriage. That's how seriously he takes it.

I encourage you again: Delight yourself in the Lord, and he will give you the desires of your heart.

Chapter Eight

On the Run

The house on the hill was not the Promised Land I imagined. The place on the mountain was a place for wandering around a peninsula of despair, just as the Israelites had done in Egypt. I imagined Greg being my Moses for so long. I imagined that he was the one to rescue me from me. By that, I mean, I believed that Greg was a knight in shining armor; in most instances, which is just what he was. Greg did take care of me and my boys very well. Now, things were changing. Something was upsetting the apple cart. However, I was not aware of this for a long time, and had it not been for a work colleague, I do not know when I would have discovered this prevailing news.

Our oldest son, Gregory M. (also referred to as little Greg), who usually would be ripping and running, had begun to complain of stomach pain, which he described as excruciating. Little Greg was quite a bit of an exaggerator as well. I checked to see if what he said was factual or an embellishment. Like most children, little Greg loved and thrived on receiving attention from those around him. I considered it to be one of his favorite pastimes. On one occasion, I can vividly remember little Greg soliciting the pity of the neighbor for food. He was born prematurely at thirty-six weeks. He weighed a whopping four pounds and eight ounces. He lost twelve ounces following delivery.

For little Greg to eat, he had to have a nasal gastric tube placed into his stomach via his nose to receive food. He did not have the proper sucking technique to sustain life; hence, he needed help. Being a mere child of eighteen years old when I had my son, I was such a novice. I knew that he would be significantly bothered by this device placed by the medical personnel to help him. I asked the physicians if they would please pull the tube out and let me work on feeding him. Although they felt it was best to keep the NGT, they did honor my wish. I took great strides with little Greg and was able to bottle-feed him. Drinking his milk took fifteen minutes to get him to drink two ounces, but he did it. Mealtime was a significant accomplishment for me and him. Little did I know that we would experience many more medical achievements from then on.

Little Greg was born with a congenital malformation termed Hypospadias. This anomaly found in boys is a presentation of the incorrect opening of the urethra that may be in the wrong place, such as on the underside of the penis. Greg would have six surgeries between the ages of two and eight. Naturally, this was a very stressful time for all of us. The repair of the malfunction took several stages. Six stages, in total, completed the process. I was working as a respiratory therapist at a community hospital during the majority of the surgeries. I never left little Greg's side for one day or night during every surgery. I showered at the hospital, ate there, made friends with other parents, and made my life there. Staying in the hospital was not challenging because it was my duty and obligation.

The last surgery that little Greg had was an unexpected appendectomy. He came home from school one day complaining of severe stomach pain. He was eleven years old and in the fifth grade. I took pride in my ability to understand my children. The innate ability to communicate well with my two boys made me feel special. We were seemingly always on the same page. When little Greg told me he was having pain, my first thought was to believe him and then investigate the nature of his misery. Upon asking him if he had visited the nurse's office in school that particular day, it would give me an indication of the seriousness of his pain.

If he had seen the school nurse, I could substantiate his claim; most children do not visit the nurse's office on bogus terms. Little Greg responded that he went to see the nurse, and she wanted him to lie down for a while to see if he would feel better. He stated that he did that but did not feel better.

I called our pediatrician for an emergency office visit and was scheduled for an appointment that afternoon. While waiting in the doctor's waiting room, I asked little Greg some preliminary questions. As the proverbial Dr. Mom, I initiated my history and physical for the patient, just as the pediatrician would do shortly. From the subjective information obtained, it was apparent that little Greg had pain in the lower quadrant of his abdomen, which radiated to his back, and these symptoms included loss of appetite. Bingo! The clincher was a diagnosis of acute appendicitis based on the description of the pain but more conclusively on the loss of appetite. After leaving the doctor's office and not being too sure about the question about his appetite, I asked little Greg if he wanted some pizza, his favorite food. I received an emphatic no! He could not imagine eating anything now. Double bingo, my son was sick; he was refusing food.

Little Greg was a bigger-than-average child, even though he was so tiny at birth. He weighed about 110 pounds and was about four feet and eleven inches tall. He was pretty healthy. I could always tell his desk when I went to the parent-teacher conferences at school because his desk was always the largest. Dr. Stone began to ask my son a little history about the nature of his pain, such as where it was and how it felt. The scale of one to ten was not a part of the vocabulary during this time. Little Greg answered Dr. Stone, and she continued with her evaluation. Partway through her examination, Dr. Stone asked Greg about his appetite. I was feeling good about my doctoring at this time. Little Greg responded to her question just as he had to mine; he had no desire. He did, however, elaborate when answering Dr. Stone that he tried to eat lunch in school but had to be excused from the lunchroom because he was feeling sick to his stomach and needed to throw up.

The examination continued with the physical aspect of the exam. Now came the time for Dr. Stone to assess whether little Greg had any localized rebound pain associated with his complaints. When a physician attempts to ascertain rebound pain, they will press rather profoundly on the site of pain and release it quickly. If the patient feels increased pain, the doctor will stop applying pressure to the site. In that case, it indicates that the patient is experiencing rebound pain and is undoubtedly having an issue of some sort in that area. Little Greg did not feel any increased pain upon the quick removal of Dr. Stones' hand; hence, she immediately established that although he was experiencing pain, this pain was not related to acute appendicitis and was being ruled out.

The physician did not confirm the nature of Greg's pain. I immediately asked Dr. Stone if little Greg did not have a response due to his size. I clarified my question by asking if she felt that the amount of adipose tissue (fat) was possibly in the way of making a diagnosis based on rebound pain. She indicated that she did not think he was a little chubby or had anything to do with this fact. I sent him to school the next day, hoping this pain would go away as quickly as it came.

When little Greg got up the next day and was getting ready for school, he said he felt the same as yesterday but wanted to attend school. I asked him again if he wanted to go to school, and he said "Yes," so I sent him. That day was to be a repeat of the day before. Little Greg went to the nurse's station again and complained of the same symptoms. This time, he came home, and I once again called the doctor's office, and Greg received an immediate appointment. Furthermore, we went to the office and, once again, re-evaluated his symptoms and, once again, gave the same statement of conclusion: pain of unknown origin. I was unsatisfied with this and knew I had to do more.

I was pretty fond of the work of a prominent general surgeon, Dr. J. Reynhout, whom I knew from the hospital where I worked. Dr. Reynhout was middle-aged, handsome, and well-liked, but most importantly, he was a skilled and knowledgeable surgeon. Because he was approachable, I had no qualms about calling his office and discussing little Greg's case with him. Dr. Reynhout did not do surgery on pediatric patients as the norm. Still, because I asked him to, he decided to evaluate Greg. I brought little Greg in to see Dr. Reynhout, and he sent him for an X-ray. I explained to Dr. Reynhout that little Greg had gone to his private pediatrician on two consecutive days, and I was not satisfied with the outcome of either of the visits. I explained how both appointments were inconclusive in establishing the cause of the pain little Greg was experiencing and that we were hopeful that he would be able to draw some definite conclusion about the pain.

The x-ray results revealed that little Greg had a condition termed a Fecalith. A Fecalith is a concentration of dry, compacted feces in the intestine or vermiform appendix. Little Greg was admitted to my hospital for the removal of his appendix the next day. Big Greg was away on business in Indianapolis, Indiana, for a meeting with the pharmaceutical company. I had been keeping him abreast of all that was happening, and now I had to call him to inform him he needed to come home because little Greg was going to have surgery. Big Greg was not scheduled to come home for another two days, but he cut his work business short and flew home immediately that same day. Not only did Big Greg come home, but his manager, Bill, came along with him to be supportive of our family as well. Bill was only in town for a few hours and then flew home to Pittsburgh.

Big Greg was a fanatic for weight control. He was fat as a child and worked hard to maintain his ideal weight. Greg was six feet and three inches tall and weighed between 200 and 215 pounds. Greg would work out wearing plastic bags to help with water loss and increased weight loss. He would take the big black garbage bags, cut a hole in the top large enough to fit his head through, and then cut two more spots to hold his arms. Once he had completed this alteration of the garbage bag, he would then put on a sweat suit and start his workout. Greg was always looking for ways to keep fit. He was always on a diet. He was always watching his weight.

When I saw my husband, Greg, come into little Greg's hospital room, I was thrilled to see him. He looked beat. He did not look like he felt all that good, but I assumed he was tired. After all, he had been away from home for almost a week and had to come home immediately and deal with all of this. I was sure he was exhausted.

One of our terrific friends, Helen, also worked at the same hospital and came to check on me and little Greg. She knew that Big Greg was away and was unaware that he was back. Little Greg had a private room, one of my few perks, and was lying in bed drifting off to sleep when Helen entered the room. I was happy to see her, but before I could say anything to her, she aimed her eyes at big Greg, focused on him, and asked him what he was on. I remember feeling stunned, shocked, aggravated, confused, and bewildered all at the same time. What was she talking about? Was she out of her mind, asking Greg something like that? What was she thinking? Why would she attack her friend and my husband as she did? What was going on? I felt as though I was watching a tennis match with only one player because I was the only one turning my head in disbelief at the statements she had made.

Finally, Greg spoke and replied to Helen's inquisition with a simple but emphatic, nothing. However, that was not good enough for Helen. My head was still going back and forth like a pendulum out of control as she asked him again. Again, he answered her angrily and said nothing. Helen was now angry and told Greg that he should tell me what he was on. She looked at me and said she would see me later. Storming out of the room, she left abruptly. I was still watching the tennis match in my head while wondering what had just happened. Before I could ask Greg what Helen was talking about, he, too, decided that he was through for the night and he was going home.

We lived about thirty minutes north of the hospital, so I knew it would take a little time for Greg to get home. About one hour passed before he called me at the hospital and told me he had something to say; he told me he had an addiction to Crack Cocaine. That is all he said, and he hung up the phone. Shocked, stunned, and surprised could not adequately describe my demeanor at this time. My world was starting to crumble, and I had no prior knowledge of anything.

Scriptural Response

What's done in the dark will come to the light.

This is how I learned this scripture growing up. I equated this to mean that secrets held by others that may or may not affect you personally will soon come to light. However, after growing in grace and studying the Word of God for myself, I was able to not only find the scripture, but I was able to learn and quote the scripture correctly. Many times, we take scripture out of context because we don't read the Bible. Rather, we simply listen to what others tell us. While that may not always be wrong, the scripture is misquoted. It is wrong.

Luke 12:2–3 (NKJV) reads as follows:

"For there is nothing covered that will not be revealed, nor hidden that will not be known. Therefore, whatever you have spoken in the dark will be heard in the light and what you have spoken in the ear in inner rooms will be proclaimed on the housetops."

Sometimes, we are perplexed by things hidden, like secrets kept. When we are kept in the dark with our life issues, we feel defeated. We feel overwhelmed and even less than. However, the Lord is gracious to us. Secrets tear us down, but the Word lifts us up! I had to hold on to what the Lord was telling me—that in spite of my troubles and my current situation, He would never leave me or forsake me (paraphrased). Deuteronomy 31:8 (NIV) helped me during the struggle. "The LORD himself goes before you and will be with you; he will never leave you nor forsake you. Do not be afraid; do not be discouraged."

These are the scriptures I had to hold on to when I was feeling nothing but loneliness. God helped me!

Part Two
I TRUST GOD

Chapter Nine

I've Had Some Good Days

As I reflected on my days of splendor with Greg, I remained lost as to how this addiction could happen. I also tried to recover lost days and remember why I was unaware of any inconsistencies in the relationship. After all, Greg always succeeded in paying the bills or taking care of every aspect of his responsibility. The trash was always put out as scheduled. The cars were being maintained with the same rate of attention as always. So how could I have missed such a significant change? The change that could have been more noticeable to me was the unfortunate notion that I had to contend with.

I tried to remember some inconsistencies; any inconsistency would suffice. If I could find at least one, I could self-treat my problem by chalking this up to a considerable need to suppress the hint of a problem. However, I was not able to think of anything. Greg seemed to come and go on the same predictable schedule as ever. There was no change in any of his habits or in the way he acted. I knew nothing. Everything was behind the veil, hidden from me.

Following the unveiling, Greg made use of his self-issued get-out-of-jail free card. The issues were freely broadcast, and I was indeed made aware of every aspect of his addiction. Becoming transparent was somehow liberating for Greg and led to frequent episodes of him disappearing from home; from the family. Now I was distraught. I was feeling isolated. I was isolated because I did not want to tell anyone. I did not want the upstanding family to be negatively judged. I did not want my children to feel less than their friends. School is difficult enough when situations are *normal*. Bullying and negative peer-pressure are heightened when students face adversity. Our new little family was already in bondage in the home with the one who promised to always protect us; allowing my boys to suffer outside the home was more than unconscionable.

Greg's newfound confession was more than a lock and key system to wreak havoc in all of our lives; it appeared as though it was his way of seeking help as loudly as he could. At least that is what I thought. As the days, weeks, and months passed, our struggle became more pronounced and more devastating to handle.

Our lives prior to this were very regimented. My role was inside the home. I took care of laundry, cooking, and shopping for the boys. My biggest role was helping little Greg with his homework every night. Greg took on the responsibility of managing the affairs related to the home (paying bills, upkeep of the cars, maintaining the yard, and being an amazing dad). Hands down, Greg was an amazing dad. I can remember one time when my oldest son wanted to be a Ninja for Halloween. The costume had to be made of cloth, with the face covering made of cloth, too. Whatever little Greg wanted; little Greg received. The very thought of his dad buying a plastic costume with a specialized hair follicle width elastic band to hold on a mask was not an option. Not an option for Greg. Only the very best, and usually the more costly item is what he would purchase for his firstborn.

At last, Greg made it home in time for the trick-or-treating adventure. My son had the costume of his dreams; he had his Ninja costume with face mask, and attire included. Little Greg was unapproachable after seeing the costume due to him jumping all over the living room, as if someone had lit him on fire. Happy was a severe understatement. Content was now the look on his dad's face.

All of this was short-lived, as Greg once again became increasingly absent from the home. The bewitching hour of five o'clock quitting time, now extended into recreational overtime. I found myself putting the two boys to bed and then sitting in the living room waiting for the car lights of Greg's car to approach the driveway. On some nights, I remember sitting there for hours. On another night, the sun would wake me up. He was not coming home. My depression and feeling of complete loneliness had exceeded what anyone should encounter. I was in a very dark, deep place.

During this time, I was still working on obtaining my four-year degree. I had been working on my four-year degree in pre-med for eleven years now. I was accustomed to the perpetual start-and-stop process of securing my degree. Nonetheless, I was bound and determined that I would get this degree and apply to medical school very soon; that was my hope and my ultimate desire: to become a physician.

Becoming a physician had been a desire of mine since childhood. My mother was seemingly always stricken with some ailment requiring intervention and the management of all those around her. For the most part, I was the person who was around. Following my parents' divorce, I lived with my mother full-time and visited with my dad only on Saturdays. However, I would have the pleasure of seeing him on Sundays at church; this was great. This arrangement was similar to the standard setup at the time. I did not particularly like or care for this arrangement, but no one ever asked me what I would have wanted or, for that fact, what I would have preferred.

Due to my mother's ongoing health issues, which mainly consisted of flare-ups of arthritis and colds, I was always required to fetch her medications and make endless pots of tea. During this time, at the young age of ten, I developed a charting system for my "patient" to keep all of her demands in check and on the appropriate schedule. Today, when I work and go to a chart, I often think about how long I have been keeping medical records and updating charts on patients' conditions.

Because of my continued desire to apply for and be admitted to medical school, I persevered to get my undergraduate degree. I was attending school at the State University of New York at Buffalo in Buffalo, New York. I was pregnant with my second son, Austin. I was working a full-time nightshift commitment as a respiratory therapist in a massive 800-bed facility, Buffalo General, all while attending classes at the university.

During this time, I met a very inspirational and soothing individual, Dr. Howell. Dr. Howell was my physiology instructor and was the most brilliant woman I have ever had the pleasure of meeting. Something about her just emitted an aura of both enthusiasm and ability. She would come to be my mentor and friend. Dr. Howell worked tirelessly at selecting my courses according to the instructor rather than by choosing the class I would take. This was possible because I was classified as an independent major, which had the implication of me being able to take all the required courses while taking the classes I wanted to be granted a degree from the university.

As I struggled in school because of so many things sitting on my plate, I never lost sight of the fact that God would help me reach my goal. I believed this with all my heart, soul, and mind. Trusting God for anything and everything was what I was accustomed to. He had never failed me, and I did not expect Him to start. I believe in God.

After the birth of Austin, as described earlier, I should not have been happier. Well, the opposite was true. I so longed to be pregnant that I developed a moderate case of postpartum depression following the birth of Austin. This pregnancy was so perfect that I always joked to my friends that I could be a surrogate mom if every pregnancy went as uneventfully as this one. This, indeed, had been a straightforward pregnancy. My hair was perfect. I did not gain too much weight. I felt so healthy. I felt blessed, and the glow in my face showed this. My picture would have been inserted if a book could illustrate the perfect pregnancy.

My oldest sister, Harriet, traveled across the country from California to be with me for six incredible weeks. Having her with me was beautiful. Because I did not have a relationship with my mom, Harriet often filled this real void for me. This was a massive void from time to time, and Harriet, who did not have children, did an excellent job filling this void. All in all, Austin was a good baby. He slept well and ate well. He brought much joy to our home. Shortly after the birth of Austin, I was ready to sit for the Medical School Admission Test (MCAT).

The MCAT was designed to weed out those students who wanted to be admitted to medical school from those who just had a desire to go but were considered incapable of handling the curriculum. The test comprised questions from every natural science category; writing and analytical aptitudes were also tested. I felt so honored to be in the room with so many students who, just like me, were hoping to perform well on this long and excruciating test just to be counted worthy of applying to medical school.

The test was ten hours long, and I thought it would never end. During the lunch break, I was joined by Greg and my two sons for lunch. I remember our picnic lunch very vividly. Lunch consisted of precisely what I requested. We dined well on peanut butter and jelly sandwiches, chips, bananas, and milk. I requested this. I wanted to eat sparingly because I had to finish the test.

I remember Greg bringing a blanket for us to sit on. The grounds of the north campus of the University of Buffalo were stunning. The trees seemed to whistle from the smooth sailing of the light wind rustling through the tree branches. I remember the sun shining in such an extraordinary way. The heat emitted from the sun was not too hot; the heat was like that of a warmed towel next to your skin after exiting the shower. It was engulfing. I felt God in this feeling. I was happy and overwhelmed. I was pleased because my three guys shared this experience with me. I was overwhelmed because I was considered worthy to sit for this exam. How particular was this time? How special was this day? How unique was God? God, the deliverer of the desires of one's heart.

Scriptural Response

PSALM 42(NKJV)

As the deer[b]pants for the water brooks,
So pants my soul for You, O God.
2 My soul thirsts for God, for the living God.
When shall I come and [c]appear before God?
3 My tears have been my food day and night,
While they continually say to me,
"Where is your God?"
4 When I remember these things,
I pour out my soul within me.
For I used to go with the multitude;
I went with them to the house of God,
With the voice of joy and praise,
With a multitude that kept a pilgrim feast.
5 Why are you [d]cast down, O my soul?
And why are you disquieted within me?
Hope in God, for I shall yet praise Him
[e]For the help of His countenance.
6 [f]O my God, my soul is cast down within me;
Therefore I will remember You from the land of the Jordan,
And from the heights of Hermon,
From [g]the Hill Mizar.
7 Deep calls unto deep at the noise of Your waterfalls;
All Your waves and billows have gone over me.
8 The Lord will command His lovingkindness in the daytime,

And in the night His song shall be with me—
A prayer to the God of my life.
9 I will say to God my Rock,
"Why have You forgotten me?
Why do I go mourning because of the oppression of the enemy?"
10 As with a [h]breaking of my bones,
My enemies [i]reproach me,
While they say to me all day long,
"Where is your God?"
11 Why are you cast down, O my soul?
And why are you disquieted within me?
Hope in God;
For I shall yet praise Him,
The [j]help of my countenance and my God.

Not only did I learn to recite this Psalm throughout my struggles, but I also relied on other scriptures to help me get over this trying time. Remembering that the LORD gives us the desires of our hearts was equally comforting. So, with that, I held onto how the LORD promised that if we take delight in Him, he will give us the desires of our hearts.

PSALM 37:4 (CEV)

Do what the Lord wants, and he will give you your heart's desire.

What does the LORD want? What does he desire? The LORD wants us to acknowledge him and to trust that no matter what we are faced with, He is more than able to deliver us from all trouble. Even when the troubles seem insurmountable, even when we cannot find a way out, and even when our backs are against the wall that we cannot breathe, even though we were facing forward without any obstruction to our faces.

PSALM 34:19 (NLT)

The righteous person faces many troubles, but the Lord comes to the rescue each time.

As I continued on in my struggles, just as you may be in the middle of a devasting time of your life, I want you to know that the Lord is more than able to deliver us from ALL of our troubles. How the LORD presents our rescue comes in different ways. The thing I am learning about how Jesus works in our lives is not typically the way we expect Him to do so. The LORD has an amazing knack for throwing curve balls into our situations. He has a way of doing the unexpected. He makes things that are crooked straight again. So, all of those really messed up areas of our lives that we try so hard to fix but can't, the LORD steps in.

Chapter Ten

I've Had Some Hills to Climb

Following the time of sitting for the MCAT was the initiation of a downward spiral. One of the most ironic things about this time was that I was looking forward to putting the disruptive and uncomfortable situations in my life way behind me. However, this was different from how things were to turn out. Not yet anyway.

Shortly after my overwhelming feeling of accomplishment for taking the admissions test to enter medical school, the sour notes played like a fiddle in my life. The disturbing part was that this life musical piece was not my choice. Greg made the most difficult phone call of all to his manager to inform him that he had a substance abuse problem and needed to seek help. Bill, Greg's manager, was seemingly very concerned and behaved very genuinely as well. Following the phone conversation between Bill and Greg, Bill asked to speak with me.

Being employed by this particular pharmaceutical company brought many perks. Although Greg was away up to ten days every forty-five days, the company recognized the stresses placed on the family units and attempted to make up for the inconveniences. Spouses would receive elaborate gifts to ease the discomfort of missing so many days away from their partners. While this number of days may not seem like much, this time was, in fact, an overabundance of time away from me and the boys, and this was an overwhelming time for us. Greg was not just the dad and husband; he was an efficient caregiver, support manager, and captain of the team in our home.

My mind and emotions continued to play disastrous tricks on me. I moved from feelings of depression and isolation to a superhighway of humiliation and devastation. I no longer liked me. I no longer liked much of anything. I was now moving around like a wide-awake, emotionless zombie. I continued to ask myself, "How could someone who was so frugal with money and selective with household purchases become so uncaring about our very lives?"

As I continued to work twelve-hour nightshifts, Greg readily took on the extras. He seemingly enjoyed the additional responsibility he encountered because of my work hours. Greg never complained; he wanted the idea of family and what this idea stood for. Even when Greg had to coach little Greg's softball team when Austin was still in a playpen, he continued to do what was needed to care for both boys. Greg would pack up Austin's playpen, gather all the snacks and bottles that Austin would need during the game, and be off to the park. Once he arrived at the park, Greg would always find a pinch-hitter sitter during game time. He would instruct the adopted sitter where he would expect them to sit (the sitter was never the same person) during the game so he could still keep an eye on Austin. Once the sitter and Austin were all secure, Greg could coach a team of little boys excited about playing softball. Greg had to go about it this way because disappointing anyone was not his nature. If there was any way possible to help anyone, Greg could be totally relied on to extend that help. Greg was not a husband unable to function without the aid of a wife. On the contrary, Greg was the most capable person I knew in the face of adversity. He prided himself on being competent. He was an excellent dad; he was a more excellent husband.

Greg was now buckling under the pressure of his recent encounter, drug addiction. His encounter presented a defeat. He was now recognizing himself as a failure. No longer was he the young man who withstood the challenges of his classmate Eric in his high school business law class. He was not winning. He was not first. No one was clapping for him now. He was spiraling fast in a downward position.

When Greg ended his conversation with his manager and gave me the phone, his manager told me that this would be the most challenging thing I would ever encounter but I would survive. These words were very comforting to me and for me.

Greg entered the best substance abuse rehabilitation clinic in the area where we lived. This program was a twenty-eight-day treatment program. His company paid the entire bill: twenty-eight thousand dollars.

I was still working the night shift when Greg was admitted to the rehabilitation clinic. I could not continue to work nights due to the lack of someone to care for my children. Greg's family, who had always supported me my entire life, was now seemingly very bitter and not helpful. I did not believe the bitterness was directed at me. His family was upset because of the loss of their son, their brother, their uncle, and their cousin. No one was going to elect to help me with babysitting needs now. This caused more devastation for me. More stress was piled on with no relief in sight. My only source of help was now in need of help himself. I was at a total loss for how to proceed. I had never been in a place to fend for myself. Greg was ALWAYS on his job.

Greg's family had by now pretty much withdrawn from the entire situation and offered me little, if any, help with the boys. The only thing I could do now was pray for another miracle. I would need one of my coworkers to switch shifts with me. Since I worked the night shift, I would have to find someone who was very understanding and willing to swap working the prime shift days with me and agree to work nights. I could think of no one in their right mind willing to do this for anyone. Although this shift paid more, working nights was a tough shift simply because of the hours. I often recalled that God never sleeps or slumbers. In the wee hours of the night, when I often dreamed about being in bed, I still had many hours to work. The night shift hours complement the day shift. Hence, the day shift hours were from six in the morning to six thirty in the evening. Likewise, the night shift would run from six in the evening to six thirty in the morning.

Working days were obviously more desirable for many reasons. One of the main reasons was the weather we encountered in Buffalo, New York. During the summer months, therapists who worked days would enjoy having four days off every week, allowing them to do many things. This was important and a perk because the summers in Buffalo were notoriously short. Another reason for wanting and desiring to work the day shift was having a greater chance of making it home after work due to snowstorms. Working nights were precisely the opposite. The therapist still had four days off, just like the day shift therapist, but at least a day and one-half of that time could not be counted because of sleeping. I had to pray to God a lot and convince a therapist (who was not yet selected) to swap this time out with me. Although I only needed to do this for thirty days, finding someone was still a bit of work.

My supervisor, Carolyn, let me know that she could not honor my request to switch shifts for two immediate reasons. The first reason she stated was due to short notice, and the second reason had to do with staffing. But, she said, if I could find someone who would be willing to switch, that would be okay. Seemingly, everything I was facing was difficult. Nothing at this point in my life was going to be simplistic. Struggle, stress, and weightiness were my new norm. Really, how much more could one person stand? Yes, enough should have been enough! After regrouping, I decided to ask God for guidance and direction.

The one therapist I was instructed, by the Lord, to ask was friendly. Even though she was friendly and good-natured, I was hesitant to ask. Working up the nerve, I walked directly towards her, boldly, to make my request. My asking should not be confused with boldness. The closer I got to Joanne, the more withdrawn I became. I was feeling like a cowardly lion on my way to see the Great and Wonderful Oz, possessing a lack of courage. The ask was not an exchange for one shift, but for a month of shifts—twelve days!

As Joanne and I made eye contact, the walk towards the Great and Wonderful Oz became more difficult with each step. I mustered up the courage to just say what I needed to say. "Joanne, I have a huge favor to ask you."

She responded by saying, "Sure, what is it, Alicia?"

Nervously, I did all I could to continue the conversation. Joanne was not just my first person to ask; she was my one and only person to ask! Without stating the reason for my needs, I just blurted out my question.

"Joanne, I need to work the day shift, and I want to know if you would consider working my nightshift hours for one month. Would you be willing to do this for me, please?"

Without taking a breath, Joanne replied emphatically in the affirmative, saying she would indeed make the switch with me. At that point, I knew God had not forsaken me, even though I was in a low state.

My family was more willing to help me out with the kids by watching them during the day and after school. This was an enormous help. I was now feeling like I had a little breathing room.

Not much, but more than I had in the days gone by. I continued to work the day shift while Greg was in rehab. We spoke a few times by phone, but not often. Those in this facility were not allowed visitors. The thought was that visits would be too distracting for the clients in rehab. Without question, this was the longest twenty-eight days in my entire life.

On the twenty-eighth day of discharge, Greg came home and called his manager immediately. This was not to be a very comforting phone call this time around. The company decided to end its relationship with Greg and terminate his position. This news was devastating for him; the news was devastating for me. What would we do now? I could not support a family on my salary. We, after all, had just purchased our second home and doubled our mortgage payment. What were we going to do? How would we survive this? Why would the company only go through such an expensive endeavor to terminate Greg following treatment? These were just a few of the many questions we had. These were the questions to us, the questions to our God. We were lost.

I had to hold onto the passages in scripture that spoke about God being my help. I was reminded of how much God loved me and would never forsake me. I needed to think about, day and night, how vital knowing God was and what I learned as a child. I waited for God to hold my hand and walk me away from this situation, as he did in elementary school. I believe in God. I did not know how or when my help would arrive, but I knew that help would come.

During this time, I did not feel supported by his or my church family. I had feelings of abandonment. I experienced feelings of disappointment, loss, and despair. Where was Jesus to comfort me?

Scriptural Response

PSALM 91

1-13 You who sit down in the High God's presence,
spend the night in Shaddai's shadow,
Say this: "GOD, you're my refuge.
I trust in you and I'm safe!"

That's right—he rescues you from hidden traps,
  shields you from deadly hazards.
His huge outstretched arms protect you—
  under them you're perfectly safe;
  his arms fend off all harm.
Fear nothing—not wild wolves in the night,
  not flying arrows in the day,
Not disease that prowls through the darkness,
  not disaster that erupts at high noon.
Even though others succumb all around,
  drop like flies right and left,
  no harm will even graze you.
You'll stand untouched, watch it all from a distance,
  watch the wicked turn into corpses.
Yes, because GOD's your refuge,
  the High God your very own home,
Evil can't get close to you,
  harm can't get through the door.
He ordered his angels
  to guard you wherever you go.
If you stumble, they'll catch you;
  their job is to keep you from falling.
You'll walk unharmed among lions and snakes,
and kick young lions and serpents from the path.
14-16 "If you'll hold on to me for dear life," says GOD,
  "I'll get you out of any trouble.
I'll give you the best of care
  if you'll only get to know and trust me.
Call me and I'll answer, be at your side in bad times;
  I'll rescue you, then throw you a party.
I'll give you a long life,
  give you a long drink of salvation!"

The overarching idea of this Psalm is how God protects us when we cleave to Him in love. Embedded in this passage is all that I was facing sadness, the affirmation of my (wavering) faith, and remembering the words of the LORD. In my sadness, it was necessary for me to hold on to the fact that I had the protection of the Lord, even in my distress. The importance of recognizing how much the Lord loved me, then and only then did I find comfort. I can now look back and recreate the message from the first verse in this Psalm, which speaks about living under the shelter of the almighty. I was constantly looking for comfort. Meatloaf, mashed potatoes, or the best dish of ice cream would suffice. I found myself becoming more withdrawn as the long days and nights encircled my personal habitat—my spirit. Finding the words of Psalm 91 brought me the solace and peace I was unfamiliar with. Reading a scripture for years is so different than becoming the one in the text. The Lord protected me from my thoughts of despair. Oh, how I love the Lord.

PSALM 92 (NASB)

It is good to give thanks to the Lord
And to sing praises to Your name, Most High;
² To declare Your goodness in the morning
And Your faithfulness by [a]night,
³ [b]With the ten-stringed lute and [c]with the harp,
[d]With resounding music on the lyre.
⁴ For You, Lord, have made me joyful by [e]what You have done,
I will sing for joy over the works of Your hands.
⁵ How great are Your works, Lord!
Your [f]thoughts are very deep.
⁶ A stupid person has no knowledge,
Nor does a foolish person understand this:
⁷ When the wicked sprouted up like grass
And all who did injustice flourished,
It was only that they might be destroyed forevermore.
⁸ But You, Lord, are on high forever.
⁹ For, behold, Your enemies, Lord,
For, behold, Your enemies will perish;
All who do injustice will be scattered.
¹⁰ But You have exalted my horn like that of the wild ox;
I have [g]been anointed with fresh oil.
¹¹ And my eye has looked at my enemies,
My ears hear of the evildoers who rise up against me.
¹² The righteous person will [h]flourish like the palm tree,
He will grow like a cedar in Lebanon.
¹³ Planted in the house of the Lord,

They will flourish in the courtyards of our God.
¹⁴They will still ^[i]yield fruit in advanced age;
They will be ^[j]full of sap and very green,
¹⁵To ^[k]declare that the Lord is just;
He is my rock, and there is no malice in Him.

I was a good math student. All types of equations fascinated me, but the equation that I most enjoyed solving was the simple equation with one variable. Equations such as $4x + 1 = 17$. I was intrigued by finding the unknown. This was the same for me when holding onto what God promised to be for me in Psalm 91: shelter. The equation I had in mind was not solved until I began to reread Psalm 92. What I knew was that prayer was important. After all, this was direct communication with our Lord and Savior. I was acutely aware that prayer produced a relationship with our God. However, I was lacking a very important variable in the spiritual equation. I was missing Praise! Humans react to joy and happiness when we see or receive good things. It is one thing to window shop and dream about having that "thing." It is another thing to have the "thing in your possession." Well, that is what I was missing in my equation of a true relationship with the Lord. My original equation looked like this: Prayer $(x) + 1 = $ Relationship. However, I discovered that my missing variables and equation components were Praise$=(x)$ and $+1$ represents patience. So, Prayer (Praise) + Patience = True Relationship.

Psalm 92 delivers a message of praising the Lord. I had to learn that. I was, like many others, really experienced at giving praise once I received what I was praying for. But in reading this Psalm, David, the Psalmist, reminded himself of how great God is, was, and continues to be. He praised and worshiped in spite of any lack. I was struggling in this area, but I soon learned that praise was so necessary. Even if we don't see the evidence of what we are hoping for, we can believe that the Lord always is our protector. Amen!

Chapter Eleven

Sleepless Nights

After Greg graduated from rehabilitation, he started spending less time at home and eventually stopped coming back altogether. Consequently, my own depression worsened, and I found it increasingly difficult to cope. I also experienced many sleepless nights. I realized that I needed to seek help to deal with my own emotions and function better throughout the day. I could no longer just get by as I had before, and I knew I needed to create a more soothing environment for myself.

The sleepless nights were caused by many things, but mainly I felt insecure and hopeless. Previously, I could push through each day and then crash at night after going through my mental checklist. I felt completely defeated. It was as if I were standing in a room filled with people yet feeling completely isolated. I became withdrawn and unsociable, avoiding going out and seeing anyone except for those I had to encounter, such as my children, people from church, and work.

I found myself in need of professional help, specifically from a psychiatrist. I was feeling very low and wondered if I might have a mental health issue. Unfortunately, our society does not treat mental health concerns with the same understanding and support as physical health problems. There is a lot of stigma and judgment surrounding mental health. I wished for a less stigmatized condition, such as a mild heart problem, so people would sympathize with me more. The idea of being under the care of a cardiologist seemed more socially acceptable than seeking help from a psychiatrist. When people see a cardiologist, they are more likely to offer prayers and support, while seeking help from a psychiatrist often leads to avoidance and social isolation.

I found my monthly visits to the psychiatrist quite daunting. They were nothing like what I had seen on TV. Instead of lounging on a sofa, I sat in a chair and answered the same questions each month.

The doctor's questions often revolved around my current medications, which I found interesting given that he was the one prescribing them. I suspect it was a way for him to assess my medication adherence.

During this time, my two youngest sons were struggling to cope with the on-again, off-again nature of Greg's situation and how it affected them personally. If Greg managed to stay sober for three days, it would give the boys a false sense of security, making them believe that all their problems had disappeared. However, this was far from the truth.

Living on a secluded road allowed me to become familiar with the cars and trucks that passed by on the street. I was able to decipher whether the passing car was from someone who lived in the neighborhood or someone driving slower looking for a cut-through to a different destination.

What really would disturb my peace was watching my two younger sons kneel in the window seat in the living room, conversing with one another as car lights approached the window, and a large glimmer of hope would embrace their faces in hopes that this car would be their dad coming home! This glimmer of hope quickly turned to dismay and disappointment when the car did not turn into the horseshoe driveway but instead kept straight down the road. I soon nicknamed my watchful, hopeful, and disappointed sons "the puppies." Doing so in a twisted way gave me solace. How? I really can't explain, but it did. You see, while I was trying my best to care for my boys holistically, I needed to care for myself as well! You know the lecture you always hear just before takeoff. Yes, the one about the oxygen mask. We are always reminded that in the event of a loss of cabin pressure, the oxygen mask will fall from overhead. The flight attendant continues to inform all passengers to be sure and place the mask over our heads *first* before assisting others. Hence, we deal with so many of life's issues. We are constantly seeking ways to self-help first, so we can then help those who need our help.

Following the time, I took the MCAT was the start of a downward spiral for me. It seemed as though every dream and aspiration I had of ever becoming a physician had vanished. The years of caring for my mom during her many illnesses while practicing medicine were seemingly done for naught, as it now appeared I would not enter medical school. This, after all, is the only thing I ever wanted and dreamed of doing. I would now have to do what I thought was inconceivable: continue as a respiratory therapist.

Being a respiratory therapist was not unpleasant; it was just a bridge or a segway to reach my ultimate goal. I was now becoming very disillusioned and slightly withdrawn. I was withdrawing from life. Only a few things I did today were enjoyable. I cared for the children, my husband, the cares of the home, and all else that incorporated my now mundane and boxed life. I no longer felt I had the bright, futuristic life I long dreamed of. Probably for the first time in a very long time, I did not feel the very presence of God surrounding me.

Around this time, I noticed the ever-present images of the *footprints* in the sand depicting God holding those who would allow Him to walk alongside them and occasionally carry them. I would have to read this poem a few times before the meaning of the words took hold of me and gripped my mind and spirit. Now, I could rest assured that God cared for me better than I could know. I was still, however, despondent. I was like a child who was told they would get a reward if they kept up with their chores. I felt as though I had kept my end of the bargain; I did my chores, and I did them well. The only problem now is that I did not see the reward. I worked very hard, multi-tasking, to accomplish all that I would need to do. I did not let anything go missing. This is what I thought, anyway. However, I needed to be corrected.

My marriage was quietly suffering. I, who was endeavoring to become a physician, did not recognize the ever-present illness in front of my face. I was so interested in taking the Oath of Hippocrates that I forgot about the oath of my marriage vows. This oversight was not intentional; I did not recognize a problem. Everything was functioning rather fine—a little scattered and hurried occasionally, but functional.

Soon, I would realize that my life was severely falling apart, and I needed to do anything to get it back on track. What I previously thought would be the solution, placing Greg in a rehabilitation center, was no solution. Rehab was putting a band-aid on a wound that needed a tourniquet.

Scriptural Response

LAMENTATIONS 3:14-26 (NIV)

I became the laughingstock of all my people;
they mock me in song all day long.
¹⁵ He has filled me with bitter herbs
and given me gall to drink.
¹⁶ He has broken my teeth with gravel;
he has trampled me in the dust.
¹⁷ I have been deprived of peace;
I have forgotten what prosperity is.
¹⁸ So I say, "My splendor is gone
and all that I had hoped from the LORD."
¹⁹ I remember my affliction and my wandering,
the bitterness and the gall.
²⁰ I well remember them,
and my soul is downcast within me.
²¹ Yet this I call to mind
and therefore I have hope:
²² Because of the LORD's great love we are not consumed,
for his compassions never fail.
²³ They are new every morning;
great is your faithfulness.
²⁴ I say to myself, "The LORD is my portion;
therefore I will wait for him."
²⁵ The LORD is good to those whose hope is in him,
to the one who seeks him;
²⁶ it is good to wait quietly
for the salvation of the LORD

Sticks and stones may break my bones, but words are enough to throw one overboard! Not always do the traditional sayings fit the lives we live. As you can see, I altered the infamous saying a bit to show how I was feeling. Horrible. Insignificant. Dismayed. I felt like a complete failure. There was no way I could imagine feeling any lower. I was on the road to doing better. I was once again slapped in the face with distress. I was lamenting within my spirit. As you read this scripture from Lamentations, reflect on the times you may have felt this way that Jerimiah describes. What helped me? I was helped by reading further down into the text with verse 22. Although I was feeling so low, by the time I got to the 23rd verse, I remembered that great is the faithfulness of the LORD. No matter what you may be feeling or how others may make you feel less because of your situation, I promise you that "the LORD is good to those whose hope is in him." Continue to trust the LORD for what you need. He promises never to leave you or forsake you. Can you hold on? Deliverance is right at your fingertips. Struggle must take a back seat to encouragement and ultimate deliverance. God is awesome! God is great! God is so much bigger than your struggle.

Get up! Walk in your deliverance. Walk in your healing! You are never alone, nor have you ever been alone. The LORD is right there with you.

Chapter Twelve
Breaking Point

I started believing in God early in life. I was introduced to the mighty, unique, excellent, and loving Lord. Even though I was keenly aware of all of this, I was still suffering in my personal life. I was doing all I could to rebound from the many losses I had faced. The twelve-step program reminds us that we have to first know we have a problem before we can be helped. From all the help I had tried to get, it wasn't enough; I needed more help. There is always a breaking point in our lives. My breaking point had finally come.

The winter months in Buffalo offered significant challenges for driving. Because I worked so far from my home, about twenty-five miles, the snow would often cause my travel time home to double. My small Volkswagen would invariably become challenged to follow the road because of the rutty fives made by more oversized vehicles. These ruts in the road were deep and icy. Needless to say, I was always on pins and needles when driving, praying I would not get stuck or run off the road. I focused on the road while driving as best I could to safely get home to my boys.

Greg's bouts of leaving home and being gone for days on end were becoming unbearable. I was always worried about how he would survive the brutal weather. Was he still alive? Had he been attacked and left dead somewhere? I always slept with one eye open during his out-of-the-house adventures. I was always happy to see him whenever he was gone for long periods of time. I would always thank God for bringing him back home. Back home to his family.

Working those long twelve-hour shifts at the hospital, three to four times a week, was more than I could handle anymore. I felt myself becoming more and more emotionally detached from life, my patients, and my faith. How much longer would I be able to hang on to the *hem of his garment?* I was quickly losing all hope.

Following the four days that Greg had been away from home, I lost all hope and all patience. Greg was roaming around in blizzard-like conditions. I remember fixing dinner and then putting the kids to bed. I walked into my room and sat at my desk to call my dad. "Come get me!" is what I said to my dad. He asked me what was wrong, and I could not muster more than "Come get me!" I hung up the phone, then fell face down on my bed, sobbing. I gathered myself, got off the bed, and again called my dad. My stepsister answered the phone, and when I asked to speak to my dad, sobbing quietly, she told me he was gone. I asked her where he had gone. "To the airport," she said. Gloria told me that my dad left the house without a coat or luggage after speaking with me.

My dad was on his way to get his baby girl. Oh, how he loved me. My dad, while excellent, was illiterate. He could not read or write. I had to find out what airline my dad was on. After very lengthy negotiations with the supervisors of each airline that flew to Buffalo from Albany, there was finally an override to disclose information on the manifesto. I now knew what airline my dad was on. I met him at the gate and drove home.

I finally was able to tell my dad about Greg. He was shocked. He was devastated! Everyone loved Greg. We decided to leave the following day and head to Albany. We left before Greg returned. Arriving in Albany finally provided the respite I so desperately needed. I was being cared for and loved. As were my children. We were out of the situation that caused me such heartache. I rested at my dad and stepmom's house and began looking for employment. I was blessed to secure a director's position in respiratory. The kids settled in, and all was well.

Three weeks after starting my new position, Greg moved to Albany. He found employment, and we started working again in a new place. We soon moved from my dad and stepmom's house and got our own place. Without fail, things spiraled out of control again. Trouble followed me. My respite had ended. All hell was once again breaking loose. To make matters worse, I was pregnant. After the birth of my second baby, the doctor informed me that the chances of having another pregnancy without the aid of fertility drugs would be like winning the lottery in four states simultaneously. I did not win the lottery in any state, but I was pregnant. Yes, I questioned God. I did not understand why he would add more pressure and responsibility to my already overfilled plate. This was not the worst thing that happened. Once again, the opportunity for rehabilitation reared its ugly head. I was so over this.

Transformation

Following the birth of the baby boy, David, life continued to be up and down. All the things that could have gone wrong, did go wrong, I left the hospital four hours after my shift ended while working in the pulmonary lab, accompanied by the nursing supervisor, two hospital security guards, and two police officers, all because I wanted to talk to someone. Out of desperation, I made a phone call to a crisis center to speak to someone. My major mistake was saying I no longer wanted to be here without clearly delineating what I meant. You guessed it right. My statement was taken out of context, leading the crisis worker to believe that I was going to commit suicide. Nothing could be further from the truth. I no longer wanted to be sitting at work with no possibility of getting home— home to my boys, not taking my life.

The time away from home would be extended by my admission to a locked behavioral health unit in a neighboring hospital. The ambulance ride was an even greater mental struggle. I was placed in the ambulance and secured with four-point leather restraints. I had now reached the lowest part of my life. I had no hope, no one to speak for me or help me. What was I going to do now?

Soon after being brought in, I was placed in my locked-down unit and instructed not to go within fifty feet of the door. I was in a mental health hospital, a mental health jail. Many of the workers asked me why I was there. I told them what happened when I called the crisis center, and they immediately said that was my first mistake. Wow is all I could think. Obviously, physical healthcare, for which I had worked all of my adult life, was inappreciably different from mental health care. After three days in "lock-up," I was at my wits end. I just wanted out of there. I became more depressed after finding out that, because I was admitted involuntarily, I would be a patient for a minimum of thirty days!

I remember crying out to the Lord in my scantly furnished private room with a tin mirror. I pleaded with him for help. I was locked up and locked in, but my faith was resurrected. Over and over,

I asked the Lord to help me. Once again, I wholeheartedly believed in God. I was unsure how he would do it, but I was confident that my prayers would be answered. My oldest son came to see me and told me my middle son was despondent. He was so sad that he could not convince him to come inside the house. He coined the phrase, "Go to Hollywood." Simply put, he asked me to figure out how to convince the staff that I needed to be released sooner than thirty days.

Just before being transported to the facility, I was admitted to the psychiatric room in the emergency department of the hospital where I worked. I was there for some time before a bed was found for me in a behavioral health facility. My children and daughter-in-law were in the room with me during the wait. Still no Greg. Why was I being punished for simply wanting to go home? Why was the Lord not helping me? Not rescuing me? What sin had I committed to deserve this harsh treatment? During the waiting press, the Department of Social Services came in because I had two minor children that would need to be placed. Before the lady could complete her sentence to say that the children would need... Andrea said she and my oldest son, little Greg, would take the children.

The entire atmosphere and environment of the facility were unfathomable to me. I never imagined anything like this. People were walking around, either humming or talking to themselves. Some would whisper, while others would speak just a little lower than a shout. Yet others walked around in a structured pattern, usually in circles. However, my most memorable memory was when the nurse would call out, in a stern and commanding voice, "Medication." I would watch in awe as each resident would line up to get their little white medicine cup of meds and show proof that they were taken by opening their mouths wide.

When my turn came to get my medication, I was immediately aware that I was given meds that were contraindicated. How could this be? After all, this is still a medical facility. Were the regulations somehow different from what I was accustomed to? Med reconciliation was always performed for new patients. I was in a dilemma. To be considered compliant, I would have to take the medication or be classified as non-compliant. Lack of compliance in taking medication would extend my time served. I knew that taking the combination of medications was detrimental to my health. I was now in a serious Catch-22.

The next day, I asked to speak with my case manager, Betty. Betty was a middle-aged, stout Black woman who I was hopeful would hear me out about the medical situation and help me. Help me get the medication order corrected, and better yet, help me get paroled. She did hear me out, but she did not carry enough weight to do either of the things I was hoping she could. What Betty was able to do was let me know I needed to speak with the physician's assistant (PA) assigned to my case. Absolutely, I would be thrilled to speak on my behalf.

Two days went by before I was able to speak with her. She was rude and abrupt. She wanted to know the nature of my request to talk to her. I responded quickly, given the lack of hospitality exhibited in her office. I explained to her which two medications were contributing to a negative outcome due to their incompatibility. She looked at me with disdain while asking me, How on Earth would I know that? I looked her directly in the eyes and told her that she knew my background in healthcare, plus I was very familiar with the two medications. She dug around in a few books, then finally looked up at me again, and in the lowest voice she could muster, she said, "You're right." Being right only changed the medication to the appropriate medication; it did not provide me with a get-out-of-jail-free card. Depression hit me hard again. I continued to pray. One of the staff members informed me that I was being watched, and if I wanted to get out of there, I would have to: 1) eat and 2) participate in the groups I was assigned to.

I immediately went into action to do the things he told me I would need to do. I should not say how awful the food was, but it was probably worse than terrible, if possible. The food trays would come to the unit on a cart with each patient's name on their tray. I would watch as others scarfed their food down and left. Once the patient returned their tray to the cart, I exchanged it for theirs. I would smile nicely when I got accolades about how well I ate. I was in Hollywood and would be more than just nominated for an award; I would win. I also attended my group therapy. Still, there was no conversation about my early release. I had to leave to go back to work and pay my bills. Staying for thirty days could cause homelessness.

I again met with Betty, my case manager, and was told my discharge date had not changed. I hurried to my room, fell to the floor, and cried. I lay on the floor because I was trying to find a way to get lower than the floor. After all, that is how I felt. Just being on the floor did not represent my true feelings. I was thinking that my situation was more aligned with the sub-flooring. While down there, I pleaded with the Lord to HELP ME! The orderlies came in and demanded that I get off the floor, or I would be in a lockdown situation. Could a lockdown be any more inhibiting than my current *locked-in* situation?

While I was wallowing on the floor, I heard the Lord say He was going to get me out of this situation. I listened to the Lord's voice as I heard him say he would walk me home! I got up off the floor on my own, lay on my bed, and began to thank the Lord for what He was going to do! On the next day, day six, I saw the facility psychiatrist. The psychiatrist was middle-aged, bubbly, and kind. He came to do an evaluation and let me know the best news ever. I will be going home tomorrow. The Lord arranged for me to go home!

Scriptural Response

PSALM 71:12-21 (NIV)

Do not be far from me, my God;
come quickly, God, to help me.
[13] May my accusers perish in shame;
may those who want to harm me
be covered with scorn and disgrace.
[14] As for me, I will always have hope;
I will praise you more and more.
[15] My mouth will tell of your righteous deeds,
of your saving acts all day long—
though I know not how to relate them all.
[16] I will come and proclaim your mighty acts, Sovereign LORD;
I will proclaim your righteous deeds, yours alone.
[17] Since my youth, God, you have taught me,
and to this day I declare your marvelous deeds.

¹⁸ Even when I am old and gray,
do not forsake me, my God,
till I declare your power to the next generation,
your mighty acts to all who are to come.
¹⁹ Your righteousness, God, reaches to the heavens,
you who have done great things.
Who is like you, God?
²⁰ Though you have made me see troubles,
many and bitter,
you will restore my life again;
from the depths of the earth
you will again bring me up.
²¹ You will increase my honor
and comfort me once more.

This is my closing scripture, my benediction. It was the start of how I once again welcomed the idea of feeling and being blessed. The Word of God tells us that what we say, it shall be. It may have taken me a little while to get to this point, but I found strength in God. Once I realized that I could not do this alone. Then, and only then, did morning come. Yes, "weeping may stay for the night, but rejoicing comes in the morning" (Psalm 30:5b).

Take as much time as you need to allow the scriptures to minister to you. Go back through them again and again. This is not just a *good read;* this is a ministering read. I shared this secret with you, not for any notoriety, but because I wanted to share that I understand how devastating life can and will be from time to time. And in all of life we face, God is our hope, our only hope.

Now unto him that is able to keep you from falling, and to present you faultless before the presence of his glory with exceeding joy, to the only wise God our Savior, be glory and majesty, dominion and power, both now and ever. Amen.

JUDE 1:24-25(KJV)

Epilogue

This book contained a secret that I kept hidden for many years. I made the choice to keep my secret because it was hurtful. The Holy Spirit had been speaking to me for years about writing this book and sharing the information. God is never wrong. Writing this book has been healing. The purpose of the book is to help the readers understand how to overcome their secrets and live a full and trusting life in Christ.

The responses following each of the chapters have been inserted to help you learn from the Word of God how to move past your secrets. Your secret may not be mine, but how God helped me to move forward is contained in the responses I shared from specific scriptures. Plant yourself in the context of the chapters while thinking about your story's point of view. The story did not end, like a fairy tale, where everyone lived happily ever after. Rather, the story depicts how awesome God is and how loving God is towards us.

From the Book of Job, we are reminded that the second half of his life was better than the first. However, we are first reminded of the beautiful life Job experienced prior to the incredible and unfortunate devastation. While I did not lose everything, like Job, I lost what meant everything to me. I lost my husband, my prince charming, after twenty-seven years of marriage to death.

As with Abraham, the Lord provided a ram in the bush for me. The ram's name is Keith. Keith and I were married at our home in Chandler, AZ, in 2013. Since my marriage to Keith, my king, I have been called to be a pastor. We opened our church, Refuge Temple of Prayer, in Chandler, AZ, in 2021, during the pandemic. Both my husband, Deacon Simpson, and I have been working together, obeying the call of the Lord.

About the Author

Dr. Alicia Michelle Simpson

Pastor Simpson, or Dr. Alicia Michelle Simpson, was called upon by the Lord to the ministry at sixteen years old and answering this call was second nature. She answered her call to Pastor during the pandemic. While things were closing, Dr. Simpson believed in God and was further drawn to helping His people. While the world was seemingly shutting down, God was using Rev. Dr. Simpson to tell the world that God was all-powerful, all-knowing, and very present during such a dark time.

Rev. Dr. Simpson has been able to continue the Lord's work and enhance the ministry of Refuge Temple of Prayer by incorporating unique characteristics of the ministry. These extra qualities include helping the homeless overcome food insecurities by providing food, hosting Bible Study in the park for individuals who do not feel comfortable coming to church, and praying with individuals who may otherwise never have an opportunity to meet a clergy. Dr. Simpson brings the church to the people.

Dr. Simpson, with a keen understanding of the needs of school-aged children, has established the Academy for Leaders, a tutoring center. This initiative, which provides tutoring to all school-aged students in grades 1–8, with a focus on Black and Brown children, is a testament to Dr. Simpson's commitment to not leave any child behind. The impact of this initiative on the community has been profound, as it is helping many children who have unintentionally been left behind in a society that promotes not being left behind.

Dr. Simpson, in her commitment to inclusivity, has established the Arizona Coalition of Women Preachers, an alliance to support women in ministry. This nonprofit organization is dedicated to serving the often-unnoticed women in ministry through workshops, small group meetings, and one-on-one mentorship. Dr. Simpson's alliance is a beacon of support and encouragement, emphasizing the importance of women in ministry and inspiring us all to do more.

With a background in healthcare and a doctorate in health administration, Pastor Simpson is an avid ally in assisting individuals in reaching their educational goals, not only in the secular world but also with the Lord. Educating God's people with bible studies, Sunday school classes, creating teaching guides, and even making a course called "Bible 101." Pastor Simpson is here to help His people learn and understand biblically based teaching for themselves.

Along with full-time pastoring and counseling, Dr. Simpson is a full-time elementary school teacher. *The Secret is Out* is her first book.

Made in the USA
Columbia, SC
31 August 2024

40832954R00055